Finally, the ancient secrets of the apostles are being revealed. These end-time mysteries were in the epistles all the time. Daniel 12:4 says knowledge shall *increase* in the last days. This last day's revelation will help you experience the supernatural as normal, just as Jesus and the apostles did!

—Sid Israel Roth
Host, *It's Supernatural!*

How do you tell someone that this is the next level of heavenly revelation and all are invited to step in? Please come and take your place at the table. If you read this book by Dr. Candice Smithyman, you will have a greater understanding of how to live victoriously and go to the next level of heavenly revelation.

—Angela Greenig
Founder, Angela Greenig Ministries
www.angelagreenig.com

Dr. Candice has poured out her alabaster box of revelation to teach the world how to access and manifest the eternal realm here in the earthly realm. In generosity she has made the reality of heavenly portals accessible to the entire body of Christ, showing the path to access full inheritance. This book is full of transformative truth from the heart of Dr. Candice, forged in the fire of God. I encourage every reader to be excited in engaging these truths. Your life is about to change as you live fully and forever from God's eternal realm!

—Rev. Dr. Betty King
Senior Pastor, TruthVine Church, London;
Founder, Bathshan Foundation

In *Heavenly Portals,* Candice Smithyman will teach you a whole range of new concepts for walking in freedom, peace, power, and prosperity, to name just a few. An eye-opener! A brain shifter! A must-keep guidebook, all for living the ascended life from a heaven-is-where-I-live-now perspective! Get this book. And while you're at it, get one for a friend.

—STEVE SHULTZ
FOUNDER, ELIJAHSTREAMS

Through His work on the cross Christ not only saved us from sin and death but also gave us a beautiful new heart and seated us with Him in the heavenly realms. This wonderful book is an invitation to partner with the Holy Spirit and see things from this divine perspective. It will help you discover what has been made available to us in Jesus and step into it, receive it, and then release it!

—GEORGIAN BANOV
PRESIDENT AND COFOUNDER, GLOBAL CELEBRATION AND GCSSM ONLINE SCHOOL; AUTHOR, *JOY! GOD'S SECRET WEAPON FOR EVERY BELIEVER*

So many believers feel limited by the natural realm. They don't realize their position in heavenly places, seated far above all principalities and powers. That's why I'm so excited about Dr. Candice Smithyman's brand-new book, *Heavenly Portals.* Your eyes will be opened to see that you are not limited by your circumstances but can walk in the power of the Holy Spirit everywhere you go and in your everyday life. Jesus is limitless, and as citizens of heaven we can walk in His limitless power and glory. We just need to change our perspective. Throughout her book Dr. Candice has powerful prayers and activations you can pray that will bring the presence and glory of God. I know that you will have encounters with God as you read this book!

—Jackie DuVall
Associate Producer, *It's Supernatural!*

Heavenly Portals by Dr. Candice Smithyman is a one-of-a-kind book that will equip all believers to access and acquire supernatural protection, provision, and God's prophetic promises. The author provides biblical, sound teaching, testimonies, and glory encounters that offer readers divine protection by which angels and heavenly beings can come and go, without demonic interference. God has designed gateways, pathways, and realms for every believer to ascend and descend by faith in the spirit to the throne of God to release heaven on earth for healing, deliverance, miracles, breakthrough, and revival.

—Dr. Hakeem Collins
Prophetic Voice; International Speaker;
Author, *Unseen Warfare*

WHERE ETERNITY IMPACTS
YOUR PAST, PRESENT,
AND FUTURE

Heavenly Portals

CANDICE SMITHYMAN

CHARISMA HOUSE

Visit the author's website at candicesmithyman.com.

Cataloging-in-Publication Data is on file with the Library of Congress.
International Standard Book Number: 978-1-63641-050-0
E-book ISBN: 978-1-63641-051-7

22 23 24 25 26 — 987654321
Printed in the United States of America

"For I know the plans I have for you," declares the Lord, "plans to prosper you and not to harm you, plans to give you hope and a future."

—JEREMIAH 29:11, NIV

This book is dedicated to my Lord and Savior, Jesus Christ, whose love and glory fill me daily. I also dedicate this book to my wonderful husband, Adam Smithyman; my three beautiful children, Alexandria, Nicholas, and Samantha; their spouses, Avery Smithyman and Hunter Lisenba; my grandchildren, Asher Smithyman and Lily Grace Lisenba; and my loving mother, Joan Borland Rainsberger.

Contents

Foreword

W E ARE LIVING in an extraordinary chapter of history. As we see the global shaking among the nations and darkness in society, it is clear that the world is broken and desperate for answers. This is not the time to throw in the towel—rather, it is the time for the people of God to arise and shine as a glorious church (Isa. 60:1–2). Everything taking place today effectively shows us just how much we need heaven to invade earth.

For the past two thousand years the church has been praying a bold prayer. The Disciple's Prayer, also known as the Lord's Prayer, includes the decree that Jesus taught us: "Your kingdom come. Your will be done on earth as it is in heaven" (Matt. 6:10, NKJV). Whether or not we realize it, every time a believer prays these words, they are succinctly calling for the kingdom of heaven to come to earth. We are decreeing for the rule of God to be established on the earth with the same power and authority that our Father God holds in heaven. Whether in government, in our schools, in the media, or in our own homes and workplaces, we need the realities of heaven to be manifested in our world. This is part of every Christian's inheritance in Christ, but how many believers actually know how to appropriate these scriptural truths in their everyday lives?

In her new book, *Heavenly Portals*, Candice Smithyman offers an invitation for you to partner with heaven's agenda for your life and for this generation. As a member of Harvest International Ministry (our global apostolic network advancing the kingdom of God in over sixty-five nations), Candice has the heart of a reformer and serves as an encouraging voice for the body of Christ. *Heavenly Portals* shares many biblical truths with a fresh and unique perspective. If you take God's truth to heart, the Word of God promises that you will be transformed as your mind is renewed (Rom. 12:2). This book will help you activate your faith in Jesus' finished work and step into a supernatural lifestyle that is available to every Christian by the power of the Holy Spirit. Because Jesus has ascended and is seated in heaven—"far above all rule and authority, power and dominion" (Eph. 1:21, NIV)—you too can live the abundant, prosperous life of an overcomer. It is time for the church to embrace the fullness of what God has for us in this season. Jesus longs to reveal Himself in every mountain of culture as Lord and King, but it is our job, as His body, to usher in His heavenly kingdom and heaven's culture wherever God has called us. It takes faith to access heaven, and it also requires Spirit-inspired strategies to realize heaven's assignment for your life.

I believe that your life was not an accident and that God has a divine purpose for you to live out in this new era in the Spirit. God wants to reveal His eternal mystery—the hope of glory—through Jesus Christ living in you (Col. 1:27), no matter what your sphere of influence looks like. It's time to arise and shine His glory as we pull down heaven to the world around us!

—CHÉ AHN

PRESIDENT, HARVEST INTERNATIONAL MINISTRY

SENIOR PASTOR, HARVEST ROCK CHURCH, PASADENA, CALIFORNIA

INTERNATIONAL CHANCELLOR, WAGNER UNIVERSITY

FOUNDER, CHÉ AHN MEDIA

Acknowledgments

I WOULD LIKE TO acknowledge the following people:

Adam Smithyman, my beloved husband, who sacrifices the most when my time is spent on book writing and traveling.

My daughter Alexandria Knight, who edits my *Glory Road* TV show, and my daughter Samantha and her husband, Hunter, who do the graphics for my social media.

The intercessors for Candice Smithyman Ministries, who continually pray our ministry into new territories.

My Freedom Destiny Church family, who sat through countless hours of teaching on the subjects in this book.

The Charisma Media leadership of Steve and Joy Strang, among others.

Debbie Marrie, vice president of acquisitions and content development at Charisma Media, for believing in this vision and wanting to get this book into the hands of many. Also to Debbie Marrie for editing the manuscript, along with Kaitie Smith, Angie Kiesling, and many others who worked on this project.

My friend Ann Marie Kelly, with all her continued support, and the Charisma podcast and marketing teams.

Sid Roth, along with Connie Janzen and my friends at It's Supernatural! Network, which produces my show, *Your Path to*

Destiny. Their tireless efforts help me take revelation like this around the world through media.

My *Glory Road* TV producer, Dolores Rivera, and her team, who produce the *Glory Road* TV show and help it expand into new territories.

My friends and administrative support team of Smith Media Group, including Linda Kiser and Nick Bailey.

My dear friend and travel assistant, Debbi Shon, along with my beautiful sister, Debra Hodgson.

Preface

ARE YOU TIRED of reaching your breakthrough and then cowering back while the enemy wins the fight? Are you tired of pressing toward a life of trusting God and living in power, peace, and rest but never getting there? Do you want to walk in the glory of God and participate in signs, miracles, and power that will overcome the spirits of fear and death surrounding you? Would you like to know how to activate faith from your seated position of power? God has an assignment for you, but you need to understand what it truly means to be hidden with Christ in God, where you are the hope of the glory of the Lord revealed on earth.

The apostles grasped this, and they wanted us to understand it too. If this is your heart's cry, you are hungry to understand the ascension of Jesus and access the eternal realm that opens portals of prosperity and glory. Here are a few ways that understanding the ascension of Jesus will truly transform your life:

- Your relationship with Father God will become more intimate.

- You will understand how you have access to heaven every moment.

- You will realize you are a royal citizen of heaven, given power to walk the earth.

- You will understand that you have been given authority to rule in the earth realm.

- You will have access to a prosperity inheritance that can be activated in the earth.

When you understand these truths about ascension, portals will open for you on earth that will change your life. Since Jesus already accessed these realms, we must practice living in them through the portals, or gateways, He opened for us. He has called us to occupy and rule these places on earth as heavenly citizens. We have been given the power to overcome the earthly realm with the knowledge of the eternal kingdom of God at our disposal.

This new kingdom was acquired already when Jesus died, resurrected, and ascended back to heaven. These portals were opened to us in the eternal realm of heaven, but most of us don't know they exist or how to access them. When the eternal realm opens to us, so does prosperity and a release of glory.

The word *prosperity* means wholeness. It means nothing missing and nothing broken in our souls. It is often derived from the Hebrew word *shalom*.[1] People get worked up when they hear the word *prosperity* because they think they will get someone "naming and claiming" wealth without any basis. The seat of ascension and the heavenly realm of prosperity are not about that. This lifestyle of heaven is eternal. We are invited to manifest this blessing when we determine to hold our position as kingdom citizens because of what Jesus did for us through His death, resurrection, and ascension. I want to help you build a structure for understanding heavenly portals and the eternal realm of prosperity. This lifestyle of heaven will release the glory. If we want to see real change on earth, we must have a reformation. However, reformation only comes when God's people are revived and in revival and commit to ruling as kingdom citizens in the army of the living God.

Heavenly portals are gateways, or doorways, that enable heaven to come to earth and reveal itself. Sometimes they are referred to as an "open heaven." In this book I will give you the keys to opening these heavenly portals and enter the realm of eternity where dominion, power, prosperity, peace, and glory will enable you to overcome in every area of your life. Then you, in turn, will help others do the same.

Introduction

I DREAMED I WAS in the section of the zoo that houses all the snakes and scorpions. It was a zoo where you could get into the pen with the animals, and I stepped into a pen designed to look like the jungle. I sensed that I wanted to test the truths God had been giving me about His eternal power and dominion on earth. I began to roll around on the sandy ground, and I could not see any of the snakes, yet suddenly different kinds popped out one by one. I would wrestle one and think, "Whew! I am so glad I defeated that." Then I would roll over as if I were waiting for another one, first under some trees and then on some grass. One by one they would show up and hiss at me, but none of them bit me.

I would grab them off my back and throw them. As I did this, the snakes would look me in the eye. I knew I was supposed to fear them, but I viewed them as a nuisance. I kept throwing them and going back in for more of the same. I would think of my prosperous soul and how they could not get access to the soul that was full of life and believed in the fullness of the resurrection and ascension of Christ. I felt whole and complete with the power of *dunamis*[1]—the miracle-working power of Jesus Christ—inside me. I was only in the pen with the snakes because I was training my mind and body to handle their attacks when they came. I kept seeing them as having no real power but just an ugly appearance and a hiss that was supposed to scare someone afraid of death. Yet not one of them bit me.

I woke up thinking, "Wow, what a gruesome time with those snakes. But why was I constantly going back for more with them? Why was I going back in the pen of my own free will?"

Then the Holy Spirit spoke to me and said, "You were training your mind with the new truths I have shared with you about the eternal realm of prosperity of soul and walking in the ascension life. You stepped through a heavenly portal into an eternal realm of prosperity."

I knew at that moment that was exactly what I was doing, and I believe the Lord wants you to accomplish the same thing by the end of this book. Heavenly portals are gateways or doorways, that enable heaven to come to earth and reveal itself. My goal in writing this book is for you to learn to walk in realms that manifest the life-giving power of Jesus' ascension in the earthly realm. I pray that you will learn to live in the prosperity realm of soul so much that who you are in your soul—your mind, will, and emotions—has expanded beyond measure in the eternal reality of life everlasting. When this happens, you magnify the Lord daily with what He has already done for you and you live life to the fullest as though all things are eternally complete from past, present, and future because of what Jesus already accomplished for us all. When you experience prosperity of the soul, you begin to live back in the Garden of Eden, where Adam and Eve were in their state of bliss with the Father.

This realm of eternal prosperity is activated on earth and available to us today. By the time you finish this book, you will look for what is missing or broken in your life and others' lives, only to say, "That missing or broken thing is a lie, and I am full in Christ in every way!" You will establish a daily system of living by Genesis 1:27–28:

> So God created man in his own image, in the image of God created he him; male and female created he them. And God blessed them, and God said unto them, Be fruitful, and multiply, and replenish the earth, and subdue it: and have dominion over the fish of the sea, and over the fowl of the air, and over every living thing that moveth upon earth.

You will realize the benefits of the ascension life, living above the earthly and soulish realm in the real world with Jesus, where the rest and peace that He accomplished through His resurrection and ascension prepare you for a life of service and glorifying Him. These lessons open heavenly portals to the eternal realm of everlasting life, which we are to live in daily even while in our bodies on earth. You will feel overwhelmed with the power God has given you to defeat death every day. You will enter the zone of eternal life even though you have not yet died in your earthly body.

If you have known in your heart there is more but struggled to get there, this book is for you. I believe it will help you develop foundational truths from God's Word that will increase your faith and position you for a next-level assignment from God. You have been equipped through His death, burial, and resurrection. Now learn what comes after the resurrection: the power of His ascension. This power opens a heavenly portal to an eternal realm of prosperity and a release of the glory of the Lord that will bring the joy, peace, and rest you have desired. I can't wait to reveal this to you, just as Jesus shared with His disciples and is sharing with us supernaturally today through His Word and Spirit. You will fulfill the assignment God has for you on this earth and learn the power of the ascension life that opens heavenly portals!

CHAPTER 1

Heavenly Portals

BEFORE I DIVE deep into this life-changing revelation about heavenly portals and the eternal realm, you must grab hold of some terms. This way you are in one accord with me as I share these revelatory secrets. During the COVID-19 pandemic everyone had to learn new tools for accessing the help they needed. Many were able to seek medical assistance via webcam technology. After setting up a username and passcode, patients could enter the portal and access their doctor and medical information, such as lab results. Each doctor had a unique portal, so patients with more than one doctor had to remember all the codes. This example illustrates what a portal may look like in the heavenly realm. You need a username and passcode to access information on the eternal realm inside each heavenly portal.

Portals are described as doors, gateways, or entrances to a

place. From a spiritual perspective portals are doorways, or gates, to the eternal realm that activate heaven on earth. In other words, heavenly portals are doorways that enable heaven to come to earth and reveal itself. These heavenly portals have been on earth from day one, and we now have entrance to them because of the death, resurrection, and ascension of Jesus Christ. We just need to know the keys or access points for entry. We enter these portals by faith. Faith comes through knowing the Word of God. You must wash in the Word to access heavenly portals and the eternal realm. The eternal realm is accessed by knowing what Jesus did from the Word of God and believing it.

A realm is a place under kingdom rulership. All realms have authority structures that define who oversees the kingdom and the rules for living in that kingdom. This book will show you the doorways, or portal openings, and the keys that will make the eternal realm open for you.

Let us begin by understanding that we live in the earthly realm, but we are of eternity. If you received Jesus as Lord and Savior, you are a kingdom citizen because He died on the cross, rose from the dead, and ascended to give you kingdom citizenship. He is the King, and you are a citizen ruler with Him. You have access because of Him. He is the door to the kingdoms in which He wants you to rule.

> Then said Jesus unto them again, Verily, verily, I say unto you, I am the door of the sheep. All that ever came before me are thieves and robbers: but the sheep did not hear them. I am the door: by me if any man enter in, he shall be saved, and shall go in and out, and find pasture. The thief cometh not, but for to steal, and to kill, and to destroy: I am come that they might have life, and that they might

have it more abundantly. I am the good shepherd: the good shepherd giveth his life for the sheep.

—John 10:7–11

YOU ARE ETERNAL FIRST

Our eternal position is advocated from a heavenly seat. We are kingdom citizens, seated with Christ in heavenly places. *Heavenly places* is an eternal realm where no sin or death exists at all. Heaven is a life-giving place, and no death is there. In the present we live in that realm because of access through Jesus, and we are called to take up our kingdom citizenship in the eternal realm and make it manifest in the earthly realm. We are not earthly except that we have an earth suit that we live in. We are heavenly, and our spirit man is alive by faith.

> Jesus answered and said unto him, Verily, verily, I say unto thee, Except a man be born again, he cannot see the kingdom of God. Nicodemus saith unto him, How can a man be born when he is old? Can he enter the second time into his mother's womb, and be born? Jesus answered, Verily, verily, I say unto thee, Except a man be born of water and of the Spirit, he cannot enter into the kingdom of God. That which is born of the flesh is flesh; and that which is born of the Spirit is spirit.
>
> —John 3:3–6

We live on earth, but we are essentially in the eternal realm. This truth makes all the difference if you want to impact environments. You have the authority of whatever kingdom you belong to. We carry the authority of the heavenly kingdom into the earthly realm.

Adam and Eve did not need salvation until they sinned in

the garden. They were eternal citizens in the earthly realm. In Genesis 1 the eternal realm was manifested in the earthly realm as heaven on earth in the Garden of Eden. There was no sin or death. God created His garden to be perfect and spotless. There was only life. He gave them charge, or authority, over the garden and every creature in it. They did not follow authority properly because they did not understand the fullness of who they were. Even with no sin and walking in the garden with God, they were easily swayed when the enemy came to deceive them.

> Now the serpent was more subtil than any beast of the field which the LORD God had made. And he said unto the woman, Yea, hath God said, Ye shall not eat of every tree of the garden? And the woman said unto the serpent, We may eat of the fruit of the trees of the garden: But of the fruit of the tree which is in the midst of the garden, God hath said, Ye shall not eat of it, neither shall ye touch it, lest ye die. And the serpent said unto the woman, Ye shall not surely die: For God doth know that in the day ye eat thereof, then your eyes shall be opened, and ye shall be as gods, knowing good and evil.
>
> —GENESIS 3:1–5

BROKEN IN THE GARDEN

The serpent cast enough doubt in Eve's mind to make her question who she was. Nothing was missing or broken in Eve's life; she had everything. Yet the serpent made her question whether God loved her, which led her to question her identity. Sin was able to enter, and she began to question her wholeness, completeness, and fullness. Her doubt invited brokenness into her eternal wholeness of soul. She questioned God's love and her identity as made in His image (Gen. 1:27). There was no sin until she disobeyed and ate the forbidden fruit, and you know the rest of the story. That brings us to the generations of Adam and Eve, from whom we descend.

Take note: Eve was whole and complete, with nothing missing or broken and *shalom* (peace) in her soul. She lived in the garden with every need met, yet the serpent Satan made her question whether she was whole. He made her think something was wrong when it was not. He made her think an error had occurred when none had.

Welcome to our world. The enemy gains access to us when we don't rule as kingdom citizens, when we question our God-given kingdom authority, or when we wonder what is broken or missing in our lives. To ruminate on what is wrong with a situation, or broken or missing, is a tactic the enemy uses to get us to think something is not right with our minds, bodies, relationships, work, neighborhoods, states, countries, or other things. The enemy wants us to think about what is wrong, which can be termed as *critical thinking*. He uses this analytical thought process to hold us in bondage to the broken places in our minds.

Once we agree with brokenness, Satan has us. Even if there is no brokenness, we are trapped into trying to figure a way out of the mess. Our pride does crazy things, and we start fixing the error ourselves. Adam and Eve did the same thing when they would not confess their mistake to God but instead made fig leaves in the garden to cover their nakedness, which was revealed after they sinned. That is the way of lack and poverty thinking.

Why would that be lack and poverty? Isn't it responsible to assess and figure out how not to make mistakes? Yes, it is, but keep it in perspective. The Bible warns that Satan is like a lion seeking whom he can devour (1 Pet. 5:8). He often does this with thoughts of lack or brokenness. It is true that sometimes things are legitimately broken and need fixing. But if you apply the prosperity realm, then even your prayer life changes. You begin to pray *from* your assurance and authority in God's love and as a kingdom citizen who knows the will of God for the situation, not as one who needs to plead with God to fix something.

WE WRESTLE WITH THE ENEMY

> Put on the whole armour of God, that ye may be able to stand against the wiles of the devil. For we wrestle not against flesh and blood, but against principalities, against powers, against the rulers of the darkness of this world, against spiritual wickedness in high places.
>
> —EPHESIANS 6:11–12

Spiritual warfare should be a normal part of earthly life, and there is a strategic way to do this. The Lord has given us the tools to win. When we live in the eternal realm of prosperity in our souls, we can win every time.

The enemy's tactic is to get us to think we are broken and can't sustain. This kills our identity of heavenly citizenship, and though we have not lost any power, we act as if we have. We allow a stronghold of fear to form, opening us up to fear and not faith. Then we have a hard time defeating the enemy, who has no power but is just toying with us.

However, in the ascension life, we understand our authority in the eternal kingdom realm. To have true power, we must not look to ourselves for confidence but to what Jesus has already done. This truth is our foundation for accessing heavenly portals and operating in the prosperity realm. I pray this book strengthens you as I share different ways to enter portals and hold our position in the eternal realm. You must understand that although you live temporally and your body dies, when you come to know Jesus as your Lord and Savior, you are invited to live eternally in every moment.

YOUR LIFE IS HIDDEN WITH CHRIST

Since, then, you have been raised with Christ, set your hearts on things above, where Christ is, seated at the right hand of God. Set your minds on things above, not on earthly things. For you died, and your life is now hidden with Christ in God. When Christ, who is your life, appears, then you also will appear with him in glory.

—Colossians 3:1–4, NIV

According to the apostle Paul, our lives are now hidden with Christ in God. We are new creatures and no longer bound to the restrictions or fear of death that so easily encompasses humanity. Therefore, the apostle Paul implores us to set our minds on things above and not on earthly things. He wants us to live with an eternal perspective. Because of what Jesus has done, eternity is ours. Eternity is yours. It started the day you became born-again in your spirit man. When you were born again, you moved from being born of the first Adam to being born of the second Adam, Jesus Christ. As a result, you are no longer bound to the fear of death.

This realization should change how you live your life on earth. If you never die, you are open to manifest the glory of God. If you never die, fear is a waste of time and miracles are at your right hand. We are called to live in the realm of eternal life because we are connected to the life-giving power of the Holy

Spirit, who comes to imbue our spirit man. Our new eternal life should involve doing what the apostle Paul said to the Colossians.

> Let the peace of Christ rule in your hearts, since as members of one body you were called to peace. And be thankful. Let the message of Christ dwell among you richly as you teach and admonish one another with all wisdom through psalms, hymns, and songs from the Spirit, singing to God with gratitude in your hearts. And whatever you do, whether in word or deed, do it all in the name of the Lord Jesus, giving thanks to God the Father through him.
>
> —COLOSSIANS 3:15–17, NIV

We can now live as if we are in eternity even though we are on earth. Jesus knew this power; it was the kingdom of heaven made manifest on earth. This power is expressed as Christ in you, the hope of glory! The apostle Paul encourages the church to watch him as an example of living out the revelation of the eternal realm. This fullness, the mystery hidden for generations, manifests as glory when we enter the heavenly portal of prosperity (wholeness). We begin to understand that we are to live without fear of death and instead walk in the eternal realm and emit the glory of the Lord.

Paul says,

> I have become its servant by the commission God gave me to present to you the word of God in its fullness—the mystery that has been kept hidden for ages and generations, but is now disclosed to the Lord's people. To them God has chosen to make known among the Gentiles the glorious riches of this mystery, which is Christ in you, the hope of glory. He is the one we proclaim,

admonishing and teaching everyone with all wisdom, so that we may present everyone fully mature in Christ. To this end I strenuously contend with all the energy Christ so powerfully works in me.

—COLOSSIANS 1:25–29, NIV

We can be grateful to God because we will not die, and with this newfound power we will bring life everywhere there is death. The enemy does not want you to know you have entered the portal of eternal prosperity in heaven; he wants you to think you are temporal, which means only saved until you die and your body is buried on earth. This is a temporal mindset, but we are called to have an eternal, or heavenly, mindset. If we fall for that lie, Satan can toy with us. We must believe the truth that what Jesus did was sufficient to give us life everlasting, and it begins today. If we grab hold of this truth, we are very dangerous to the devil's schemes in the earthly realm.

ETERNAL TIME PORTAL

Ecclesiastes 3:1 says, "To every thing there is a season, and a time to every purpose under the heaven." Our purposes are under heaven in this realm of earthly time. That word *time* is the Hebrew word `*eth*, which means now or continual time,[1] broken down to the Hebrew word `*ad*, which means eternity or everlasting or a world without end.[2] This means that heavenly time is considered to be the predominant time plan of God. Heavenly time is eternal time. The phrases *eternal time, realm of eternal time,* or *realm of prosperity in the eternal* all refer to the eternal time that Jesus bought back for us, the space of time we lost when Adam and Eve sinned and death entered, which separated earth time from the eternal.

In the earthly realm we have restricted time. It is time on a continuum with a beginning and an end. It is not a world without end; it is the realm of set time, appointed time, season, day, and night. It is a shortened time span because death cuts into the eternal. Humans are on earthly, or suspended, time until we receive Jesus as our Lord and Savior. Then we enter eternal time, or a realm of prosperity, as a heavenly doorway opens for us. We enter a realm of time unsuspended by death that continues forever; it is a heaven and earth with no end. This heavenly portal, or doorway, is your life hidden with Christ in God. Remember, Jesus told us He is the door, or gate: "I am the door: by me if any man enter in, he shall be saved, and shall go in and out, and find pasture" (John 10:9).

King Solomon, the son of David and Bathsheba, was considered the wisest man on earth, and he authored these wise words.

> I have seen the travail, which God hath given to the sons of men to be exercised in it. He hath made every thing beautiful in his time: also he hath set the world in their heart, so that no man can find out the work that God maketh from the beginning to the end. I know that there is no good in them, but for a man to rejoice, and to do good in his life. And also that every man should eat and drink, and enjoy the good of all his labour, it is the gift of God. I know that, whatsoever God doeth, it shall be for ever: nothing can be put to it, nor any thing taken from it: and God doeth it, that men should fear before him. That which hath been is now; and that which is to be hath already been; and God requireth that which is past.
>
> —ECCLESIASTES 3:10–15

There is much truth in these scriptures about life in the earthly realm. I believe King Solomon was a scribe of God revealing the truths of the eternal realm that we otherwise would not know because we were born into earthly time. He wanted us to know how to beat the time warp of sin and death that surrounds men and women of God. They toil under the curse and can't seem to break free. How will one escape this toil and finally make it to the heavenly realm, where eternity has no beginning and no end?

> He hath made every thing beautiful in his time: also he hath set the world in their heart, so that no man can find out the work that God maketh from the beginning to the end.
>
> —ECCLESIASTES 3:11

The Hebrew word for *world* means "concealed, i.e., the vanishing point; generally, time out of mind (past or future), i.e., (practically) eternity."[3] In this passage Solomon shares that, because of sin from Adam and Eve, humanity has a concealed or hidden part of the mind where we cannot understand God's timetable for past, present, and future. He is saying that man is in a time warp of earthly time that only God knows, whereas God is on another timetable, and our minds are skewed and unable to process time from God's viewpoint. We cannot understand an everlasting life. We are unable; it is a disability we have in our souls due to the fall of humanity. Yes, we are born again in our spirits, but our souls are constantly transforming our minds into understanding eternity and the prosperity of heaven. We are in a state of lack, even a state of lack of time.

The dominion of sin, death, and the grave cripples us, which means we cannot see, feel, or experience time as God originally intended in the Garden of Eden. God intended that we be on His eternal time, but Adam and Eve were tricked into giving up eternal time for all humanity when they ate the forbidden fruit and Satan took them into a state of death. They were in life, yet Satan lied to them that more life was needed. They bought the lie and entered the very thing that was against God, which is death. God was only life, and they were His kids, intended to be only of life. But they forsook their life-giving destiny for a lie that they would live when they were already living. Therefore, humanity's search for the meaning of life is focused on eternal life and prosperity of soul, where nothing is missing or broken and we have *shalom* peace.

> Now the serpent was more crafty than any of the wild animals the LORD God had made. He said to the woman, "Did God really say, 'You must not eat from any tree in the garden'?"
>
> The woman said to the serpent, "We may eat fruit from the trees in the garden, but God did say, 'You must not eat fruit from the tree that is in the middle of the garden, and you must not touch it, or you will die.'"
>
> "You will not certainly die," the serpent said to the woman. "For God knows that when you eat from it your eyes will be opened, and you will be like God, knowing good and evil."
>
> —GENESIS 3:1–5, NIV

God knew they would die in the Hebrew sense of the word *muwth*, which means to die (literally or figuratively), destroy, or slay. It can also mean "to die prematurely (by neglect of wise moral conduct)."[4] They would become dead in their spirits because they neglected wisdom. The wisdom of Solomon begins with understanding the realm of eternal time. Eternal time is the essence that will cause us to reenter the realm of life.

Solomon wants us to know we are to gain this understanding and knowledge of God, and in doing so, we will escape the clutches of the death trap of time. He does not know of Messiah, Yeshua, who will come to set us free, but Solomon knows we must step out of the clothes of earthly time and learn to love life even amid the shortness of the earthly time warp. He says, "He hath set the world in their heart, so that no man can find out the work that God maketh from the beginning to the end" (Eccles. 3:11).

There is a divine key to understanding the eternal, and when we grasp it we will know the redemption of time. That key is Messiah, who would become our doorway to the eternal realm of prosperity. This has been made manifest for us in the life of the New Testament. However, I believe many citizens of heaven—born-again Christians here on earth—do not know all they have been given. They don't understand the importance of knowing the hidden truth of eternal time being made manifest and available to us in the earthly realm.

WISDOM FROM HEAVEN

Solomon continues, and let's reread it.

> I know that there is no good in them, but for a man to rejoice, and to do good in his life. And also that every man should eat and drink, and enjoy the good of all his labour, it is the gift of God.
>
> —Ecclesiastes 3:12–13

Can we, God's people, begin to rejoice even while toiling so that we will become the overflow of life? Can we defy the earthly time warp we find ourselves in and daily live as though that curse was broken? Solomon is giving us wisdom from heaven. And remember, Messiah has not yet come when he shares these truths. So how much more do we have now that the heavenly portal is finally open by Jesus' death, resurrection, and ascension?

Then Solomon says,

> I know that, whatsoever God doeth, it shall be for ever: nothing can be put to it, nor any thing taken from it: and God doeth it, that men should fear before him. That which hath been is now; and that which is to be hath already been; and God requireth that which is past.
>
> —ECCLESIASTES 3:14–15

Solomon says that what has been written is taking place now, and what is coming has already been. How? Because it exists in the eternal realm. He says God requires that we search out what is past or already written in the eternal realm.

What is past? The Hebrew word for *past* is *radaph*, which means to run after with hostile intent, chase, put to flight, or follow after. Used figuratively, *radaph* can refer to time gone by.[5] Let me break this down for you with all the truth stored in the words. It means, "That which hath been [eternal] is now [present earthly]; and that which is to be [present earthly or future] hath already been [exists in eternal]; and God requireth [strive in prayer and worship] that which is past [exists in eternal]." Solomon is essentially saying that God requires what is eternal.

You may be wondering how this helps you now. Shift your mind and heart to the eternal and your temporal pain will be overcome. The sting of death is gone since the eternal realm is open. Eternity was concealed in the heart of man, but now the eternal gateway has been opened by Jesus. We need to step into the place where eternity is revealed, and then we will truly begin to live on earth.

We are to fervently attempt to understand time already written in the scrolls of heaven. It is a finished work by God. It is where He is and where He will be for eternity. It is a realm of eternal prosperity, and we are called to seek it out with great anticipation so that we might find life as it was destined to be. We carry out His plans until the day we move from the earthly realm to the heavenly realm.

THE LIFE OF STEPHEN

The truth I want to share is from the powerful life of Stephen mentioned in Acts 6 and 7. By faith he entered the eternal realm to speak wisdom. Stephen was categorized as having faith, *dunamis* power, and wisdom from heaven. Just like Solomon, he is recognized for this wisdom in the Scriptures.

> And Stephen, full of faith and power, did great wonders and miracles among the people. Then there arose certain of the synagogue, which is called the synagogue of the Libertines, and Cyrenians, and Alexandrians, and of them of Cilicia and of Asia, disputing with Stephen. And they were not able to resist the wisdom and the spirit by which he spake.
>
> —Acts 6:8–10

This wisdom came from heaven by the Spirit of the Lord. But in the following verses, the Sanhedrin accused Stephen of blasphemous words against Moses.

> Then they suborned men, which said, We have heard him
> speak blasphemous words against Moses, and against God.
> And they stirred up the people, and the elders, and the
> scribes, and came upon him, and caught him, and brought
> him to the council, and set up false witnesses, which said,
> This man ceaseth not to speak blasphemous words against
> this holy place, and the law: For we have heard him say,
> that this Jesus of Nazareth shall destroy this place, and
> shall change the customs which Moses delivered us. And
> all that sat in the council, looking stedfastly on him, saw
> his face as it had been the face of an angel.
>
> —ACTS 6:11–15

Through His death and resurrection, Jesus did indeed change the customs of how Moses delivered the people because Jesus fulfilled the whole law. The Jewish people sought God only through Torah and the Ten Commandments but not through relationship with the Father through the death, resurrection, and ascension of Messiah Jesus, which opened the portal of life to us. When Stephen had defended his faith and come to his time of death, they claimed he looked like an angel. His face had changed appearance, as though this portal was so advanced it had changed the earthly realm.

> When they heard these things, they were cut to the heart,
> and they gnashed on him with their teeth. But he, being
> full of the Holy Ghost, looked up stedfastly into heaven,
> and saw the glory of God, and Jesus standing on the
> right hand of God, and said, Behold, I see the heavens
> opened, and the Son of man standing on the right hand of
> God. Then they cried out with a loud voice, and stopped
> their ears, and ran upon him with one accord, and cast
> him out of the city, and stoned him: and the witnesses

> laid down their clothes at a young man's feet, whose name
> was Saul. And they stoned Stephen, calling upon God,
> and saying, Lord Jesus, receive my spirit. And he kneeled
> down, and cried with a loud voice, Lord, lay not this sin
> to their charge. And when he had said this, he fell asleep.
>
> —ACTS 7:54–60

Stephen could see into the heavenly portal that was above him, as he says, "I see heaven open and the Son of Man standing at the right hand of God." The Sanhedrin, who had not yet believed in Jesus as Messiah, could not tap into the heavenly portal. Yet they could still sense the power of heaven being released at this moment even though they were unaware of the portal. Because it was said that Stephen's face "had been the face of an angel," even his accusers knew something was different. The accusers then stoned him, and we know Stephen was in the eternal realm at that time, as he could say, "Lord, do not hold this sin against them." When he had spoken these things, he died, and his spirit went to the eternal realm.

Stephen entered an eternal realm by faith to the point that he could face death, stand up to his accusers, and petition the Lord not to hold the sin of killing him against them. Death brings fear, but when the power of death is defeated by faith in what Jesus has done, there is no fear. Perfect love casts out fear (1 John 4:18). God sending His only begotten Son, Jesus, to save the world means that what was lost in the fall is now regained. So is access to the heavenly portal that opens the eternal realm of time. The eternal portal of life that Stephen experienced during his death is the eternal realm of prosperity that Jesus opened for us.

This portal defies death and the fear of it in our current life. We must no longer fear death or be a slave to it. Stephen did not allow fear to stop him from living by proclaiming the gospel. Now who has the power? Do we or our archenemy, Satan? We do! We have all the power, and we are called to walk in that power as citizens of heaven.

> However, we speak wisdom among those who are mature, yet not the wisdom of this age, nor of the rulers of this age, who are coming to nothing. But we speak the wisdom of God in a mystery, the hidden wisdom which God ordained before the ages for our glory, which none of the rulers of this age knew; for had they known, they would not have crucified the Lord of glory. But as it is written: "Eye has not seen, nor ear heard, nor have entered into the heart of man the things which God has prepared for those who love Him." But God has revealed them to us through His Spirit. For the Spirit searches all things, yes, the deep things of God. For what man knows the things of a man except the spirit of the man which is in him? Even so no one knows the things of God except the Spirit of God. Now we have received, not the spirit of the world, but the Spirit who is from God, that we might know the things that have been freely given to us by God.
>
> —1 CORINTHIANS 2:6–12, NKJV

This passage speaks of the hidden wisdom that God ordained before any one day came to be. We find this wisdom when we understand the portal of the eternal realm of prosperity that Jesus opened for us. We are no longer slaves to the end of time; we can daily live as though time is no longer something to beat but instead is something gained by Christ when the power of death was defeated. We have His Spirit ruling inside us with all wisdom, and He is opening our hearts daily to understand the life we carry. We have our hearts and our spiritual eyes opened to the power of life regained for us.

PRAYER OF FAITH

Lord, I pray that everything in this chapter has deposited deep into the souls of those who read. I ask You to supernaturally open the reader's eyes to know and understand what the wisdom of heaven reveals to us. As God's children, we are called to a life of eternity in the here and now. Solomon and Stephen both knew these truths about eternity. Lord, help us walk by faith into the knowledge that causes us to strive through prayer and worship to understand this realm of eternity. A heavenly portal was opened to us by faith when Jesus died, was resurrected, and ascended back to heaven, and we must apply that truth and begin to live the eternal life we have been given on earth by faith. Jesus our Messiah has made the way! We now have defeated death and the accompanying fear that causes us not to step out in faith and truly live. Lord, teach us to open these portals of heavenly prosperity and begin to live today.

QUESTIONS *for* REFLECTION

1. Now that you understand the differences between earth time and eternal time, how does this challenge your way of life?

2. Since Jesus opened a portal in heaven for you that you can enter daily by faith in the Word of God, how will you activate this portal so that you can daily have access?

3. Write one stirring question you have about the eternal realm. I believe God will answer it for you as you continue reading this book.

CHAPTER 2

Why the Ascension Life?

GOD IS GETTING ready to take His church to the next level in these last days. The Lord wants to share keys that will teach us how to live in the eternal realm. As His children we are called to live the ascension life with Jesus.

You are probably familiar with the resurrection life, and hopefully you are living it out daily. The resurrection life is the overcoming and victorious Christian life that Jesus bought with His shed blood on the cross for us. He died and rose from the dead so that we might live it! The resurrection life should be the everyday Christian life.

But how much do you know about the ascension life and the power of the prosperity realm? Have you ever heard of such a concept? It is found in Scripture. Understanding what Jesus did for us in His death and resurrection is powerful. But there is also power in the ascension because it means our position has changed. We know our position has changed because of the truth of the Word of God, and we have washed our minds with that truth. If you remember from the introduction, Jesus' ascension means that you are a royal citizen of heaven, given authority to rule in the earth realm. You daily live out your inheritance as a royal citizen because you have been given the right to access heaven every moment, and your relationship with Father God is growing daily because you know Him in His Word.

It means we are now eternal and kingdom citizens called to walk on earth. These benefits of the ascension life were acquired when Jesus robbed Satan of the power of death and God repositioned us as children of the inheritance, seated with Him in heavenly places (Eph. 2:6).

God has been ministering this truth for years, and the ascension life is rightly discerned in the Word of God. It has been there from day one in the New Testament, which reveals what happened to Jesus at the resurrection and ascension. When Jesus resurrected, He defeated sin, death, and the grave. He enabled us to be saved and live as overcomers of evil and death. The power of the resurrection means the enemy has been defeated, and we are called to live a grace-filled life. This resurrected life is amazing! However, there is more to the story. We are not just overcomers and victorious over evil; we are called to be kingdom citizens, walking in power to tread on snakes and scorpions, because we are seated with Christ in heavenly places.

This position enables us to be change agents on earth. We are called to live, move, and breathe from a new position that reflects the truth that Jesus ascended to heaven and is still there now, and He says we are also—even today. We have a powerful position, and our understanding of this position will enable us to live as though the eternal realm of heaven impacts our past, present, and future. In this book I will walk through many scriptures to reveal the truths that open portals of heaven so you can begin to put these truths into practice and watch God change your world.

For this to happen you must see the world through the power of Jesus' ascension. You must see yourself as complete and whole in your soul. You must live as though you are an eternal creature with nothing missing and nothing broken. Because of what Jesus did and the shifting of power from a focus on death to a focus on life, you can exercise your power as a kingdom citizen over the realm of death and live in the prosperity realm. This means the revival of your soul, which leads to the reformation of your world. God can use you to reform nations when you come to understand the power of being seated in heavenly places—or what I'm calling heavenly portals in this book—and how to operate in them daily in the earthly realm.

The word *ascension* in Greek is *anabaino*, which means to arise, ascend, climb, go, grow, rise, spring up, and come up.[1] Focusing on this word and the power of the ascension life is what I call "living the rise." We are rising above all things!

The ascension life is different from the resurrection life. The Spirit of the Lord supernaturally takes His children through this process to teach them to carry the responsibility of greater assignment while resting in His peace as they grow in trust of God. When God is ready to promote His people, He will teach them new aspects of His ascension.

The resurrected life focuses on living victoriously over sin, death, and the grave. This is vital in our Christian walk. However, the resurrection life is only the foundation for the ascension life. We are called to live in a way that makes a difference on earth. The resurrection life provides us with the basic tools to give God glory, but Jesus knew there was more, and He shared this with His disciples and with the world.

THE RESURRECTION BEGINS THE PROCESS

As we know from Scripture, the ascension happened after the resurrection.

> In my former book, Theophilus, I wrote about all that Jesus began to do and to teach until the day he was taken up to heaven, after giving instructions through the Holy Spirit to the apostles he had chosen. After his suffering, he presented himself to them and gave many convincing proofs that he was alive. He appeared to them over a period of forty days and spoke about the kingdom of God.
> —ACTS 1:1–3, NIV

We are told that Jesus spent forty days ministering and meeting with family and friends before ascending to the Father. He spoke certain things to His disciples during this time to let them know there was more to this life than the power of His resurrection. The promise of the Holy Spirit would open a new understanding to them and the world.

As members of the body of Christ, we want to go beyond the resurrection life and live the ascension life, because it's in the ascension that we see God doing work on earth in His glory, even when we may not be actively involved in it. We may be in attendance to a miracle but also rest, as God gets all the glory. We learn to let God be God because we have taken our position by faith. He comes to move because we have chosen to believe we are ascended with Him. The ascension life means we get to participate with God from a place of rest while He does the work in us, through us, and around us for His glory.

He becomes the power source for change as we rest in Him and His ascension grace.

As mentioned earlier, the Greek word *anabaino* means to arise, ascend, climb, go, grow, rise, spring up, and come up.[2] The ascension life is one in which we live above. We live as if we have risen to new life in the resurrection, and we go to next-level living, in which we are seated with Christ. We are rising above all things. We rise to a place where we trust God because of all He has done in the resurrection. It is a place where we grow up! Yes, we have a foundation in the resurrection, but now we are learning to rise above all things into the eternal realm of prosperity, where the ascension power rests. We learn to make a difference in the earthly realm because we have risen with Jesus into the eternal realm. Jesus is seated in the eternal realm, in heavenly places, and by faith we are too.

You might be wondering how that can be. It doesn't make much sense to you yet. Let's pray and then dig into the Word of God so you can receive a revelation of what God wants you to learn.

PRAYER FOR REVELATION OF ASCENSION LIFE

Lord, please reveal the secrets of the ascension life as we learn the Scriptures and grow in wisdom and knowledge of You. We thank You, Lord, that You are pleased to give us the keys to the kingdom of heaven that open heavenly portals through which we can see Your power manifested. We want to know these truths to participate with You as You release global glory on earth. Lord Jesus, we are ready to receive this revelation. Our hearts are hungry for more of You, and we want to know You from our position of being seated with You in heavenly places, as the apostle Paul has stated in Ephesians 2:6. We want to live and breathe as citizens of heaven first, able to tread on earth with snakes and scorpions, knowing everything has already been defeated. We want to live in the heavenly realm, where we rest on the sovereign dominion power of God, who defeated death and has given us the power to rule and reign with Him in the earthly realm. Thank You, Lord, for speaking to us and taking us to new levels of knowing You.

THE ASCENSION BEGINS

While reading these chapters on the ascension of Jesus, remember that we are ascended with Him in the spirit. Although we live on earth, we are in an eternal heavenly realm, where prosperity exists daily. We must train our minds to believe we are there in order to saturate our environments with these eternal truths. Understanding these heavenly portals begins when we recognize positionally where we are. This understanding enables us to walk by faith through gateways of power.

Your mind is the only thing preventing you from winning your battle with the enemy. Once your mind is prosperous and you are in a place of faith moment by moment, you have mastered the prosperity realm. Jesus mastered the prosperity realm, and therefore the power He had on earth was great. When I refer to a prosperous mind, I am writing about a mind that is focused on the eternal and has overcome lack and poverty. A prosperous mind thinks on things above at all times. Jesus had a prosperous mind, and we acquire this by faith and knowing the Word of God.

Jesus says we who believe will do greater works than He did (John 14:12). Why? Because He goes to Father as an advocate for us. Not only is Jesus interceding for us, but we are also seated with Him next to the Father. This means we are in the same eternal realm of power as Jesus all the time. We just don't know how to live like it. That is why I'm writing this book: to teach you to engage the eternal heavenly realm of prosperity every moment and not come out of this realm as you walk in the realm of temporal earth. The portal is accessed through a prosperous, sanctified mind that thinks on things above and the truth from the Word of God that we are seated with Christ in heavenly places.

The word *portal* means "a door, gate, or entrance, especially one of imposing appearance, as to a palace."[3] A realm is "a royal domain; kingdom" like the realm of England. It also means "the region, sphere, or domain within which anything occurs, prevails, or dominates: the realm of dreams." A third meaning is "the special province or field of something or someone."[4]

When I discuss portals, I am discussing the doors, gateways, or entrances to a place we have access to already by the blood of Jesus and His resurrection and ascension. We have the keys, and we must go through certain gateways to occupy certain realms. This book will show you the portal openings that make the heavenly realm operate for you.

FOUNDATION FOR HEAVENLY PORTALS

Your ascension begins first at the foundation of the resurrection. The truths on the ascension life begin with Mary Magdalene and Jesus at the tomb after He resurrected. Let's look at the very first encounter in Scripture that reveals what happened when Jesus resurrected.

> Now Mary stood outside the tomb crying. As she wept,
> she bent over to look into the tomb and saw two angels in

white, seated where Jesus' body had been, one at the head and the other at the foot.

They asked her, "Woman, why are you crying?"

"They have taken my Lord away," she said, "and I don't know where they have put him." At this, she turned around and saw Jesus standing there, but she did not realize that it was Jesus.

He asked her, "Woman, why are you crying? Who is it you are looking for?"

Thinking he was the gardener, she said, "Sir, if you have carried him away, tell me where you have put him, and I will get him."

Jesus said to her, "Mary."

She turned toward him and cried out in Aramaic, "Rabboni!" (which means "Teacher").

Jesus said, "Do not hold on to me, for I have not yet ascended to the Father. Go instead to my brothers and tell them, 'I am ascending to my Father and your Father, to my God and your God.'"

Mary Magdalene went to the disciples with the news: "I have seen the Lord!" And she told them that he had said these things to her.

—JOHN 20:11–18, NIV

Jesus has resurrected from the grave and is standing next to Mary Magdalene. She doesn't recognize Him, partly because she was overcome with fear. Sometimes we can't recognize when God is speaking to us because we are so overcome with grief and fear. Jesus snaps her out of it by calling her name. Then she comes to her senses. The same is true for us. When God calls our name, we finally pay attention during our crisis, come to our senses, and discern truth. Mary is talking to Jesus at this point, and He says specific things to her that show the difference between the power of the resurrection and the power of the ascension. Jesus says, "Mary, don't hold on to Me. Do not cling to Me."

Remember, the Greek word *anabaino* means to arise, ascend, climb, go, grow, rise, spring up, and come up. Jesus is saying to her, "Don't hold on to Me, as there is more to the story for Me and you, and I must rise so you can rise. I must *go* up so you can *grow* up. I must take My position in the heavenlies so you can take your position with Me." We must understand these powerful truths if we want to see our lives and culture change.

FEAR MAKES US CLING

Mary was experiencing what we all experience when something we love is lost or when we fear being alone or that death is near. She was frantic. Think of a time you were frantic when you lost something you loved. Losing something we love is like death. Death brings fear. When we lose something we love, we will cling to anything. We might cling to a person, place, or thing; it might be healthy, unhealthy, peaceful, or dangerous. We cling to it because we are afraid. If we don't know Jesus, we cling to the things of the world.

> Do not love the world or anything in the world. If anyone loves the world, love for the Father is not in them. For everything in the world—the lust of the flesh, the lust of the eyes, and the pride of life—comes not from the Father but from the world. The world and its desires pass away, but whoever does the will of God lives forever.
> —1 JOHN 2:15–17, NIV

We are people in need of a Savior, cast from the Garden of Eden, in need of provision, protection, and acceptance. We are lonely and alone. We came into the world alone, and we leave alone, but we don't have to be alone on the journey unless we choose to be. We can allow Jesus to fill that void in our lives with a deep and abiding relationship with Him. We understand that He is our Savior and makes a way for us to have relationship with God the Father. Because of Jesus' resurrection and ascension, we can rise to the place He has called us to be: with Him in heavenly places.

> Praise be to the God and Father of our Lord Jesus Christ, who has blessed us in the heavenly realm with every spiritual blessing in Christ. For he chose us in him before the creation of the world to be holy and blameless in his sight. In love he predestined us for adoption to sonship through Jesus Christ, in accordance with his pleasure and will—to the praise of his glorious grace, which he has freely given us in the One he loves.
> —EPHESIANS 1:3–6, NIV

We are blessed with blessings in the heavenly realm because of the resurrection, but we live out the spiritual blessings when we position ourselves in spiritual places. Spiritual places are the eternal heavenly realm of the ascension. It is here we will see the blessings come to pass and our inheritance realized!

MY TESTIMONY OF FEAR

We all have stories of God stepping into our lives and changing things for us. In those moments, the power of resurrection was made manifest in our lives. And once we completed that stage, God showed us there was more. Once the power of resurrection was revealed, our hearts wanted more of what the ascension could bring us. We may not have been able to articulate it as such, but it was a journey of growing into the ascended life, a need for more.

I would like to share a personal story about clinging to things because I was afraid. My father died when I was nine years old. I was in the fourth grade, and I came home from elementary school to find a house full of relatives, and I knew something terrible had happened. It was as if I had entered a temporal opening to the power of death that day. My mother came to the door and told me to follow her to this big gold chair in our family room. All these people were standing around crying. She put me on the floor at one of her feet and my sister at her other foot. Then the room got quiet, and she leaned toward me and said, "I have something to tell you. Your father has died." I let out a blood-curdling scream, and that was it. That was all the emotion this nine-year-old girl showed. I never cried. I got up and greeted everyone.

I went outside to play with my best friend, Lisa. I began to tell my neighbors the news of my father's passing on that same day as I was playing with their kids outside. Some thought I was lying and said things like, "Your father didn't die. What an awful thing to tell people." Then when some people heard the news, they said, "Raymond has gone to heaven because he was a good man." I was thinking, "A good man. Well, I need him. God doesn't need him."

Then I held in all my pain and the bad theology of well-meaning people and sucked it up. My dad was gone, and I was alone. Fear gripped my life, and demonic forebodings came on me. The portal of death was opened on a young girl, and I could not stop it. Why? Because I was broken. I did not know my identity in Christ. A serpent invaded my little Garden of Eden, and I agreed with that serpent that I was broken and might never be fixed.

I began to fall into depression at age nine, and at that time no one talked about depression. Counseling wasn't a thing in the 1970s. Three weeks later my body broke down, and I was in the hospital for six weeks with three feet of my intestines removed. I had Crohn's disease, but until the attack it had gone undetected. I lived most of my teen years in rebellion and anxiety, fear and depression, all because my father had died. I had nothing to do with his death, yet the one I loved was gone, and now this was my loss. I can relate to why Mary Magdalene was so delighted to find Jesus alive. She began to cling to him in fear He would leave again. All she wanted was Him, and all He wanted was to take Mary, the disciples, and all of us to heaven with Him. He shared this with her in the dialogue we read earlier.

My battle with clinging and fear continued. Later I married my husband, Adam, and I found myself overcome still with fear, anxiety, and depression. Adam was a lieutenant junior grade in the US Navy, and we moved to Barbers Point, Hawaii, as our first duty station. About eleven months into our new marriage, he was deployed to Japan for six months. When he left, I started grieving all over again. I was depressed and alone, living six thousand miles from my family in Virginia.

I had no idea how clingy fear had made me until Adam was gone. I was broken inside from my father's death, and it had carried over to my marriage. Fear was my friend—fear of aloneness, death, flying, heights, insects...you name it. I now know this was a combination of the underlying fear of death we all have from the fall of man and the trauma I suffered from the loss of my dad. I spent my life feeling unloved, unprotected, unaccepted, and unprovided for. I thought my husband would be my savior and be all this for me. God had another plan: to show me who my real Savior was. Praise Jesus for the resurrection that overcame sin, death, and the grave!

I remember filling the void while Adam was gone by going to the bookstore and searching in the self-help section for psychology material on why I was so lonely. I tried all kinds of remedies via self-help books and magazines; I knew the answer was somewhere. I did not think it was Jesus because I felt He was too busy with big things like wars and famine and wouldn't care about little me. Wow, what a lie from the enemy. Can you relate?

Then one day in the bookstore, I came across a book titled *Where Is God When It Hurts?* by Philip Yancey. The title struck me. Here I was in a bookstore seeking help. I was hurting, and in my heart I was sure God could help me, but would He? That book stirred me to seek a new relationship with God. I had to move from the earthly and soulish dimension of thinking to the hope of the resurrection. This was the beginning of my journey to search for the power of the resurrection. Although the terms were big for me, I was essentially doing that as I read the self-help books. It's what we all do when we first come to Jesus. We search for an understanding: Why should I know Him? Who is He, and why should I care about Him? Does He care about me? Does He even know I am alive?

This quickly progressed to questions of His resurrection power after I had a life-changing encounter with God and was supernaturally healed from fear, anxiety, depression, and Crohn's disease. The resurrection power of God was released that night when I was healed. Having no knowledge of God and the miraculous other than what I read in the Bible, I was surprised by my personal experience, as it brought me to a reality that God indeed loved me, heard my prayer for help, and was willing to heal me. The night God touched me I prayed, "God, if You're there and You can hear me, I can't get myself out of this one." What I meant was I could not get myself out of sin, death, and the grave. I was the walking dead in the flesh. I had no feeling. I was numb and sick and grieving and depressed. I needed the resurrection in my life.

Then God touched me in my sleep. My healing was from God alone. No man laid hands on me, no person spoke life to me, and no one was in the room with me when I fell asleep or when I woke to this powerful encounter of joy and peace from heaven that healed my frail, 110-pound body. His glory permeated me, and I was healed. I needed to know the resurrection power over death.

Later in my walk with God I would come to learn the ascension power as I hungered for more of His glory. However, this resurrection joy and awareness lasted a few days. Then the Spirit of the Lord spoke to me and said, "Memorize every scripture you can on the power to overcome fear, anxiety, and depression, because it will return." So I set out to do just that, and I had to fight with the resurrection power of Jesus that overcame sin, death, and the grave and its evil forebodings and lies of the enemy. It was resurrection power at its finest. I would study, stand, pray, memorize, decree, declare, and demand, and it worked! I was learning to fight with the Word, and God met me.

As these evil forebodings tried to cling to my untrained mind and senses, I would fight with the Word of truth and faith against the enemy. God was teaching me the resurrection power of overcoming sin, death, and the grave! If this was all of it, that was fine. But I knew there was so much more.

Over the years I received the baptism of the Holy Spirit and spoke in other tongues. I saw miracles and healing happen at services where God was moving. People were touched by God when no one touched them, much like what happened to me years before. I knew there was more, but how and when would I see God use me in that type of environment, and how could this become a part of my daily life instead of a happenstance? I studied and earned multiple degrees in counseling and ministry and even an honorary doctorate and earned Doctor of Ministry, but I still knew there was more. There had to be more than degrees and knowledge. I was cultivating a relationship with God that fulfilled my hungry heart, and it was more than knowledge could give me.

An understanding of the ascension was beginning to form, although I did not know it at the time. The Lord had to teach me about the earth realm, soulish realm, and spirit realm. He has done so now, and I will share them with you.

Jesus told Mary, "Don't hold on to Me," because she had to know the rest of the story. It would not have been good for her to know only the resurrected Jesus. She had to know the Jesus who ascended so she could enter His rest. In this way she would one day know Jesus as her God (John 20:17). This personal relationship would be so deep that fear, anxiety, depression, and the evil forebodings with them would forever be gone, and she would ascend to confidently rule with Jesus on the mountain. She could be in this place of peace and rest with Him daily, even while her body, spirit, and soul were on earth.

Mary tried to cling to Jesus too early, and He said no. He knew that the best was yet to come, and it involved the Spirit of the Lord being released on earth. He knew that after this happened she could go to the next level of knowing Him, the place of rest that the author of Hebrews wrote about.

For if Joshua had given them rest, God would not have spoken later about another day. There remains, then, a Sabbath-rest for the people of God; for anyone who enters God's rest also rests from their works, just as God did from his. Let us, therefore, make every effort to enter that rest, so that no one will perish by following their example of disobedience.

—HEBREWS 4:8–11, NIV

ASCENSION IS REST, PEACE, AND POWER

The ascension is the next level of rest and peace. It doesn't mean you won't fight the good fight of faith or undertake a battle; it just means your weapons of warfare are not carnal (2 Cor. 10:4). It means you fight from the heavenly realm in a seat of rest and peace, knowing God and trusting in His love. We can know that He will release what we need when we need it, and we are called to rest in this.

Ascension is a seat of power and rulership with Jesus in your spirit and soul, an eternal realm in heaven even when your body is in the earthly realm. It is a place where you know all He has is yours. It is the eternal realm being made manifest in the earthly realm. It is a place where struggle is reduced when you allow yourself to remain there by faith. Why? The resurrection was not Jesus' final resting place; it was a passing through to the next dimension of ascension.

So it is with us. The resurrection conquered the dominion of sin, death, and the grave. It opened to us kingdom dominion, but there is still more to the story. Just because kingdom dominion has arrived does not mean we have the tools to operate in that dominion. That comes with understanding the power of ascension.

Jesus is our example, as He passed through to ascension and did not come back to the resurrection. The resurrection occurred at one time to defeat death. The ascension is permanent eternity, an eternal realm we can live in daily. Jesus stays ascended and makes a place for us.

> Do not let your hearts be troubled. You believe in God; believe also in me. My Father's house has many rooms; if that were not so, would I have told you that I am going there to prepare a place for you? And if I go and prepare a place for you, I will come back and take you to be with me that you also may be where I am. You know the way to the place where I am going.
>
> —JOHN 14:1–4, NIV

He is not leaving His ascension—His seat in heaven next to the Father—and we can't either. He bought it for us with His blood, and it is also our eternal resting place.

Back to Mary and her dialogue with Jesus at the tomb. Let me paraphrase what Jesus said: "Mary, don't cling to Me here at the gravesite. Even though I have resurrected, there is more to come, and it is not about the grave. It is about life after the grave. The dominion of death is defeated, and you are called to operate and fight every day in the earthly or soulish realm. You are called to do this from the eternal, heavenly realm of prosperity, where heaven meets the earthly realm. Train yourself to respond from this place of ascension, the heavenly spirit realm, by faith in Me. Then you will get through the fight on earth."

Jesus taught Mary some keys right there at the gravesite, the place of overcoming and resurrection. He taught His disciples these same things for forty days, and then He ascended—and so can we! Jesus dropped nuggets of truth regarding the resurrection. But all the while He was setting them up with His life as an earthly example of ascension life. Because of Jesus' death, resurrection, and ascension, we have been given the Holy Spirit.

> But the Advocate, the Holy Spirit, whom the Father will send in my name, will teach you all things and will remind you of everything I have said to you.
>
> —JOHN 14:26, NIV

The Holy Spirit is our guide today to both resurrection life and ascension life.

In the next chapter I want to share some more truths Jesus shared with Mary at the gravesite. I believe they provide the foundation for living the ascension life. We are graduating from the resurrection life to the ascension life, and the Word is our cornerstone for ascending the mountain of the Lord. I would like you to join me in a prayer.

PRAYER FOR REVELATION OF ASCENSION LIFE

Lord, thank You for sharing Mary's authentic heart of fear that her Rabboni was gone and she would not see Him again. Lord, we ask that You help us identify fear in our lives. Your resurrection has given us tools to fight this fear, but even so You want more for us. You want us to go beyond fear to faith, beyond restlessness to eternal rest, and beyond the pit to the palace and peace. Teach us, Lord, the keys to the ascension life and the eternal heavenly realm of prosperity so we can experience the next level of rest, peace, and trust as we watch You release the glory into our lives and circumstances. You want us to take our proper seat of authority as the dominion of sin and death is defeated. Teach us how to do this, Father. Let us receive wisdom, revelation, and understanding so we can go to these next-level places with You, in Jesus' name. Amen.

QUESTIONS *for* REFLECTION

1. List any specific fears coming from a place of brokenness that create bondage in your life. I believe when you do this, that bondage will be defeated.

2. What habit, pattern, or person do you cling to in order to be relieved from your fears?

3. What have you learned in this chapter about the differences between the resurrection life and ascension life that can impact your daily living?

CHAPTER 3

Relationship With the Father

A S WE LEARN about the ascension life and living in the eternal realm of heaven, we must include our relationship with the Father. Jesus made a way for this relationship with Father God to grow and develop so we would have the power to rule in the kingdom. This relationship develops the bond that causes us to walk as citizens of heaven and exercise the kingdom's power with authority. Portals, or gateways, in the spirit realm open pathways to revelation, impacting how we live for the kingdom.

Let's discuss what happened after Jesus resurrected and walked the earth before He ascended into heaven. There are keys to our development as we study walking in the eternal realm on earth. One of those is to understand the encounter Jesus had as He walked on the road to Emmaus.

In this encounter Jesus was resurrected, but He hadn't yet

ascended. He was walking on the road to Emmaus when He came upon two people. Most theologians think they were two men, although only one was named. These guys didn't recognize Jesus. They were sharing about the resurrection, and Jesus listened to what they were saying.

As Jesus joined their conversation, the Scripture tells us that the hearts of these men began to burn. They had come close to the One who had resurrected. They could feel that fire burning. They knew that when they were next to Him, a revival was happening inside them. Even though they didn't recognize Him until later when He blessed the food for a meal they were sharing, on the road they felt their hearts burning when He talked with them.

> When he was at the table with them, he took bread, gave thanks, broke it and began to give it to them. Then their eyes were opened and they recognized him, and he disappeared from their sight. They asked each other, "Were not our hearts burning within us while he talked with us on the road and opened the Scriptures to us?"
> —LUKE 24:30–32, NIV

As followers of Jesus we want to be carriers of that kind of fire. We want to know Him as our Father and our God. No matter what your relationship with your earthly father, your relationship with the heavenly Father is different. It is a relationship that raises you up in ways that only God can do. God blesses earthly fathers, and He gives them great wisdom, anointing, and understanding to raise their kids, but even an earthly father needs to have his Father in heaven to help him be a good earthly father. Now, I don't know how to be a father, only how to be a recipient of God's Fatherly love, which He taught me well. As you read earlier in my testimony, I didn't grow up with a father. Yet I've seen fatherhood in action in my home with my husband, Adam, and our children.

SHOW US THE FATHER

Because I was fatherless, I had a broken place etched into my soul. As a result I looked for love in all the wrong places. I didn't know the love of a father until Jesus got hold of me. And then I came to know the love of my heavenly Father, and that love continues to grow. I ask for that love to grow every day because the more I know my heavenly Father and grab hold of His heart, the more I fall in love with Him. This is what these men on the road to Emmaus wanted.

They wanted to know God the way Jesus knew God. As the disciples watched Jesus perform signs, miracles, and wonders, they would say, "Jesus, show us the Father." And He would say, "If you see me, you're seeing the Father; I am the replica of the Father." (See John 14:9-11.)

We must ask ourselves, "Are we replicas of our Father in heaven?" We are created in His image. That's what the Word tells us. Yes, the fall of man came and corrupted that image. But when we come to know Jesus as our Lord and Savior, we reposition ourselves back to that place where we can have the purity, wholeness, and righteousness that Adam and Eve had in the Garden of Eden. And we can begin to express the heart of the Father to the world. The world is only a dying place when it doesn't know the heart of the Father. Once it knows the heart of the Father, it wakes up, it quickens. It turns into a place of revival.

Everybody who has ever been saved was in sin and had to confess. We all need to know the love of the Father and that He is our Lord and Savior. We need to know His love and His identity and who we are in Him. These are the basic needs of humanity. Many of us came to Him in a time of trial. Many of us were pushed hard before we surrendered and said, "Jesus, I need You in my life." But at that moment the Father came and rescued us, and we made God our Father.

In this season I think the Lord is rebuilding our temples so we can carry more of the glory of the Lord. He wants to shine more of His glory through His creation, but we cannot shine more until we know who the glory giver is. We can't bring forth something we don't already know.

Start asking God to show you the greatness of Him being your Father and you being His very special child. If you doubt you are special to Him, meditate on His goodness and love in the Word.

Many times we equate God's love with our circumstances. That is a danger zone. Don't go there in your mind. It's not a place you want to be. If you start looking at the things going on around you, you might become convinced that your sovereign Father doesn't love you. That quickly happened to Adam and Eve while they were in the Garden of Eden. All it took was the serpent telling them things were not as perfect as they could be, which was a lie about God, and they began to spiral down from there. If we look too hard at our surroundings and miss the truth, we will spiral down also. This is living in the earthly realm instead of living in the heavenly realm.

TESTIMONIES OF GOD'S LOVE

I have the honor of interviewing some of the top prophetic voices and leaders in the world on my *Glory Road TV Show.* One week I interviewed Dr. Bill Hamon, who has taught more than a quarter of a million members of the body of Christ how to walk in prophetic gifts. He was sharing a story about a series of challenging events that happened to him. He and his wife had multiple losses, one right after the other. You can read his testimony in *Your Highest Calling*, a book about the trials and tragedies of his life, in which he came to a place of living at peace with this one truth: God causes all things for the good (Rom. 8:28). No matter what's happened, our God can turn everything terrible, evil, or against us into something good.

The same thing happened with Dr. James Goll, whom I also had the honor of interviewing. He says the same thing in his book *Tell Your Heart to Sing Again*. No matter the trauma and loss, one of which was the death of his wife, he found hope and peace in knowing that God causes all things for the good (Rom. 8:28). Both seasoned men of faith who have lived long lives serving the Lord came to the same conclusion.

If you want to enter a place of rest with God, make that your motto in life. If you have a serious issue going on, you may say, "Look at the seriousness of what's happened in my life. Did you see what happened to me yesterday? Did you see what happened to this family? Did you see what's on the news today?" Then answer yourself with Scripture, "Wait. God causes all things for the good." You may not see the good that God is redeeming because of everything happening to you, but the Word says He's causing all things for the good.

How many times do you say, "Well, I didn't see anything good come out of that"? When you say that, you haven't seen through the eyes of God because if you had you would have seen something good. That is the earthly realm. It is a bound place where our natural tendencies are toward negativity and bondage. That is a result of the fall of man, but Jesus redeemed that. Through His death, resurrection, and ascension the realm of death has been defeated, and we now live in the realm of life, prosperity, and all spiritual blessings.

We must ask the Lord to help us live daily in this realm. We must practice this eternal realm because the earthly realm and its bondage are more connected to our souls than the freedoms of the eternal heavenly realm.

ENTER THE PORTAL OF PROSPERITY

Do you believe in the goodness of God during trials and circumstances? That's the question in every test and trial you go through. If you can maintain ascension in the middle of your crisis, you will maintain the attitude God wants you to have while going through the temporary trials and circumstances of earth.

That's what I mean by entering a portal of prosperity and peace. It is a place where we know His goodness resides, and we operate in that faith daily. We must know that He is bringing us to a place of greater good during the trial. If we can train ourselves every day—no matter that place of fear, bondage, insecurity, or weakness—to maintain a mental understanding of God causing all those things for our good, then we will have joy amid our trials. The writer of the Book of James tells us to "count it all joy" when trials and temptations come our way.

> My brethren, count it all joy when ye fall into divers temptations; knowing this, that the trying of your faith worketh patience. But let patience have her perfect work, that ye may be perfect and entire, wanting nothing. If any of you lack wisdom, let him ask of God, that giveth to all men liberally, and upbraideth not; and it shall be given him. But let him ask in faith, nothing wavering. For he that wavereth is like a wave of the sea driven with the wind and tossed. For let not that man think that he shall

receive any thing of the Lord. A double minded man is unstable in all his ways.

—JAMES 1:2–8

Yes, a double-minded person is unstable, and Eve was our evidence of that. As soon as the serpent told her something untrue, she agreed with that lie. She became double-minded and could not stand. If we don't believe in the goodness of God, we will become unstable. The goodness of God is a staple in the eternal realm of prosperity. The prosperity realm builds off of knowing that God is good all the time. Therefore, the writer of the Book of James could say, "count it all joy," amid what was going on. I'm not saying it's easy to do; it's a challenge, but that's what the Word says, right?

The Greek word for *count* here is *hegeomai*, which means to lead, command with official authority, deem, consider, be chief, govern, judge, rule over, and think.[1] This is a governmental word for the power and authority we have as kingdom citizens to defy what the natural earthly realm is saying and grab hold of what the supernatural eternal realm of prosperity is saying. We have the authority to think and count something as joyful, no matter what it looks like.

The writer of James is saying, "I know it looks bad, but as a kingdom citizen you have authority to count it all joy." We have kingdom authority through Christ to stand in the realm of a prosperous soul and have joy amid temptations and trials. This kind of authority will open the portal of prosperity so you can enter that realm, and the devil will flee. To count it all joy, to laugh amid your trial, is a strategy of war.

I will share more with you later, but this means you are not of the earthly realm because the world does not respond that way.

The world responds as if it is dying with every difficult thing. The world cries out in complaining and murmuring, in anger and frustration, but in a kingdom authority given by the eternal realm of heaven, we can respond with joy. I can't wait for you to learn more about the eternal portal of prosperity. Joy is an attribute of it!

When we talk about the ascension, we must realize the disciples thought they had lost their Lord and Savior. They had heard the stories. Jesus had walked in and said, "Listen, this is what will happen to me. I will die, and then in three days I will resurrect" (Mark 8:31; Luke 9:22). He told them all these things, but they didn't realize how weak their faith was until everything happened.

God is telling you things about who He is and about what's going on around you. You may not be in a place yet where you can receive it, but He's talking to you, He's sharing with you. He speaks in His Word, the Bible, when you pick it up and seek His heart. The whole Bible from Genesis to Revelation is a story about who He is and how He causes all things to work for our good. Now that we have established a foundation on the truth that He causes all things for good, let us continue our discussion on the ascension.

OUR FATHER NOW

In the first chapter I wrote about the conversation Mary and Jesus had at the tomb, when Jesus said,

> Do not hold on to me, for I have not yet ascended to the Father. Go instead to my brothers and tell them, "I am ascending to my Father and your Father, to my God and your God."
>
> —JOHN 20:17, NIV

Jesus explicitly says that God is not only His God but our God. He's not only Jesus' Father; He's our Father. Jesus is explaining this to Mary because He wants her to tell the disciples that His resurrection caused a completion and a finishing point.

Now the scenario has changed. Since the resurrection has occurred, we have a new relationship with Father God. We can have a personal relationship with Jesus' Father, who is also now our Father, because Jesus finished His task to go to the cross and reconcile us to the Father. Think about that for a minute. Jesus had to die, go to Hades and get the keys of death, and resurrect so that we might have a relationship with the Father.

Most Christians don't hold their relationship with God in the place that they should. And I think today many are way too casual about their relationship with God. For us to have life in Christ and a relationship with the Father, there was a cost. Jesus paid with His life. The dominion of sin, death, and the grave was broken, and we were made whole through what Jesus did. So now we, as unbroken people, can have a new life, the foundation of which is our relationship with God. That is powerful. We were pulled from death to eternal life through the heavenly portal activated by faith in Jesus Christ. We now receive all the benefits of this new foundation, including God's power inside us, in that Jesus told the disciples He would send the Comforter, the Holy Spirit, when He ascended and would go to the Father on our behalf.

PORTAL OF POWER

The resurrection defeats death and its power, but the ascension is the gateway for eternal life-giving power to come to us. Jesus says,

> And I will pray the Father, and he shall give you another
> Comforter, that he may abide with you for ever; even the
> Spirit of truth; whom the world cannot receive, because it
> seeth him not, neither knoweth him: but ye know him; for
> he dwelleth with you, and shall be in you. I will not leave
> you comfortless: I will come to you.
>
> —JOHN 14:16–18

This excited Jesus. I want you to know that. Yes, He overcame the dominion of death, sin, and the grave. This foundational first step meant that those who received salvation would also be with Him in the heavenly kingdom. However, I believe Jesus was even more excited that He would ascend because He would then send us the Holy Spirit, who would be our Comforter and friend, God living in us. I believe that was a greater joy for Jesus.

There were clear steps to this victory: His death, burial, resurrection, ascension, and sending us the Holy Spirit. These steps to salvation were decided before the foundation of the world, as Jesus agreed to this task, and the Holy Spirit had to wait a lot of years before He could come and be with us. Jesus knew we would all have fellowship with the Father through the Holy Spirit because of what He, the Son, had done.

Take an inventory of how much you honor the Holy Spirit in your life. Do you honor God living inside your body as His temple? This is why it's so important to keep your body holy, pure, and righteous. It's not so we can brag about how great we are or how we do everything right and others do everything wrong. By the way, it's self-righteousness when we do that. When our eyes are open spiritually and we see that the relationship with Him is more important than anything, we realize the fullness of Jesus' death, resurrection, and ascension. When we honor Jesus for giving us a relationship with the Father, we are grabbing hold of the gift of the Holy Spirit, who never leaves nor forsakes us. We are stepping into knowing that God is our Father. He is not only Jesus' Father but also our Father, and we are adopted.

> In him we were also chosen, having been predestined according to the plan of him who works out everything in conformity with the purpose of his will, in order that we, who were the first to put our hope in Christ, might be for the praise of his glory. And you also were included in Christ when you heard the message of truth, the gospel of your salvation. When you believed, you were marked in him with a seal, the promised Holy Spirit, who is a deposit guaranteeing our inheritance until the redemption of those who are God's possession—to the praise of his glory.
> —EPHESIANS 1:11–14, NIV

Our position has changed because the dominion of death is broken, but the good news does not stop there. We are now moved to the dominion of life and the prosperity realm. We are now back in the Garden of Eden on earth. We now live in the eternal realm of prosperity, which means we are grounded in God's love and goodness. Being seated with Christ in heavenly places means that we live *beyond* the initial step of recognizing that sin, death, and the grave have been defeated.

Many Christians don't live as if they are saved. They engage in sin daily. Even though death has been overcome, they're living as if they were still in their graveclothes. Living in our graveclothes means we are friends with fear. I know this firsthand, as you'll recall from my testimony in chapter 2. Fear is the outcome of death. Fear is the byproduct of being separated from God. When you're in a relationship with God, do you have any fear? No. So when you're with Him, fear flees. Why? Because "There is no fear in love; but perfect love casteth out fear: because fear hath torment. He that feareth is not made perfect in love" (1 John 4:18). When we are in a relationship with Him, suddenly we're not afraid. We have entered the eternal portal of heaven that impacts the temporal earth realm.

RELATIONSHIP OPENS THE PORTAL OF PROSPERITY

This key can keep your soul living the ascended life: *if you're experiencing fear, it just means you missed relationship in that moment.* If you missed that last sentence, please read it again. Fear is a normal part of humanity. It is one of the byproducts of sin and separation. As a result we've carried fear with us. From the time we are born we try to manage our fear. Some people manage it with a lot of medication. Some people manage it with sinful responses, such as fits of rage, manipulation, control, and so on. Some people want to harm something or even harm themselves. Sometimes people will throw fear on you so you can join them in the realm of fear.

There are spirits of fear that detect when we are afraid, and they come to join us in our fear. This is why it's imperative not to allow fear to take hold of you. If you've got to spend your lunch break in your car playing worship songs until you can break the fear off your life, do it. Remember, Jesus' sacrifice already broke that fear. You must enter the eternal heavenly realm now to live fearlessly. This is where you decide what's more important. Is peace more important, or is living your life in a place of fear, anxiety, and worry more important? The realm of fear and worry is part of life. But because of Jesus' death, resurrection, and ascension, we don't have to stay in that realm—that place of fear and worry. If you've been stuck there, I want you to say a prayer with me now.

PRAYER TO DEFEAT FEAR

Lord, help me deal with this debilitating fear. I know You died, resurrected, and ascended to set me free of sin, death, and fear. Help me learn to overcome, as You have done everything for me already. Help me realize this in my mind, will, and emotions so that I can live in the peace and eternal life You give to me! You shifted me to the eternal realm of prosperity. Help me live there with You.

When I write about living the ascension life, I am writing about "living in the rise." Living in the rise means living above your circumstances and trials. It is living a life where sin, death, the grave, and fear are overcome daily. This means you must learn to "live above," and you must fight to stay there. God gave that life to you, but you must fight to stay there. What I mean is you must continually train your mind to remain where He has properly positioned you in the ascended heavenly realm of no fear, not where you feel like you are. This will open you to the prosperity realm where all of God's gifts to His children are available.

TOOLS FOR LIVING THE ASCENSION LIFE

Become a master at understanding your senses. This takes some time. Many people want to be healed, but they don't want to go through the healing process or use the tools God has given us. They want to experience supernatural healing. When

I experienced a supernatural encounter with God where fear, anxiety, depression, and Crohn's disease were defeated in one touch from the Lord, directly after that encounter with God, He said, "Get in My Word and memorize every scripture you can on fear. It is going to come back." He was trying to tell me that demons were coming back for me. He had cleaned out my house, or my body temple, but my mind had to stay alert and be trained and continually washed in the Word of God. I had to hold my ascension position with Jesus in the heavenly realm of prosperity by exercising that I was seated with Christ in heavenly places.

What happens to demonic forces when God touches you supernaturally? They back off as if a bomb hit, and they scatter. But in time they creep back in. They creep back in when we use the wrong language, talk down, or talk negatively. They creep back in when we let fear steal into our minds or dwell on what is missing or not whole in our lives.

The honest truth is we don't believe that God causes all things for good, so we never move into that trusting place with God. What I am sharing is developmental training of the mind. Please feel no condemnation if I'm describing where you are. It's OK. I used to be there. Everyone is there until they learn to train their mind. The apostle Paul tells us,

> Do not conform to the pattern of this world, but be transformed by the renewing of your mind. Then you will be able to test and approve what God's will is—his good, pleasing and perfect will.
>
> —Romans 12:2, NIV

Everyone on the planet struggles with this. When you grow in mind transformation, you grow in peace.

The mind governed by the flesh is death, but the mind governed by the Spirit is life and peace.

—ROMANS 8:6, NIV

They must turn from evil and do good; they must seek peace and pursue it.

—1 PETER 3:11, NIV

Paul and Peter knew that we have to grow in peace. We have to fight for our peace continually. We must keep people out of our sphere who want to bring fear and anxiety. We must rise above them and their mess and get to the place where we know our peace. Then we can deposit peace from the Word of God on them when they need it.

A great way to break the grip of fear and depression is to go on a food or drink fast of some sort. When you abstain from food or drink for a certain period of time, the Lord will bring to your mind different areas that He is working on to cleanse and heal you. When I need to deal with issues in my mind, I go on a fast. Then God will reveal the lie I am harboring and how to counteract it with a truth from His Word. This sets me free, and I enter a zone of peace, the eternal heavenly realm of prosperity.

When you live the ascension life you are in fellowship with the Father. You will see miracles, healings, and other amazing things happen because God can use you when you're that closely connected to Him in your mind and soul. He wants this for everybody.

Very truly I tell you, whoever believes in me will do the works I have been doing, and they will do even greater things than these, because I am going to the Father. And I will do whatever you ask in my name, so that the Father

may be glorified in the Son. You may ask me for anything
in my name, and I will do it.

—John 14:12–14, NIV

We know that we can do greater things because Jesus
ascended to the Father and sent us the power of the Holy Spirit.
And when we pray from our heavenly ascension seat in Jesus'
name, the Father will be glorified because of what the Son did,
and we will receive because every promise in heaven is yes and
amen in Him (2 Cor. 1:20).

THE FATHER'S HEART OF PROSPERITY

Let's study more about the Father's heart in Luke 15, the story
of the prodigal son. I want to teach you something about the
portal of the heavenly realm and the power of ascension in this
passage.

The younger son ran away from the father and left his home
in pride. He was stubborn. The Word tells us something happened to him while he was out there in the world. He had
no provisions, no food, and he was eating out of pigpens. He
thought, "My God, the servants eat better than I do! What was
I thinking?"

When he came to his senses, he said, "How many of my
father's hired servants have food to spare, and here I am
starving to death! I will set out and go back to my father
and say to him: Father, I have sinned against heaven and
against you. I am no longer worthy to be called your son;
make me like one of your hired servants."

—Luke 15:17–19, NIV

Repenting and returning to the Father is coming to your senses. Verse 20 says, "But while he was still a long way off, his father saw him and was filled with compassion for him; he ran to his son, threw his arms around him and kissed him."

That's the prosperity realm, the life of ascension. That's the heart of the Father. He has compassion on us and runs to us, throws His arms around us, and kisses us—even when we screw up, make a thousand mistakes, or get angry with Him and say things to Him that we wish we hadn't. The heart of the Father is compassion and love. The father responded to his son the same way he did when he gave the son all the gifts before he ran off and squandered them. When the son returned he didn't beat the son a thousand times and say, "How could you have done this? Look what you did to me!" He did not take it personally.

How many humans respond from that perspective? Most of us say, "Look what you did to me when you made this mistake. This is all about me." The father didn't say that. Do you know why? Because he represents our heavenly Father, who is constant and never shifts His position based on circumstances. Like the Father, Jesus is the same yesterday, today, and forever (Heb. 13:8). He lives in the heavenly realm where every spiritual blessing is. He is in the prosperity realm because He is ascended.

Even when His children shift, the Father does not shift. He knows that He is love. He knows that He is just and that He is merciful. He knows about His greatness. He knows all these things about Himself. He doesn't have to convince us of those truths. He doesn't get offended. He knows His identity, and He loves us too much. He created us for His joy, His pleasure, and

His love. He wants His children to reflect His glory, as they are the hope of His glory!

THE LORD DISCIPLINES

When the Father sees us come back to Him, He wraps His arms around us. That kind of response is the heart of the Father. Luke 15:18–19 says that after the son receives such love and mercy in the father's response, the son says, "Father, I have sinned against heaven and against you. I am no longer worthy to be called your son." That's a heart of repentance. How can a heart repent like that? Because one knows the Father's heart of love. The love and mercy of the Father draw us into a place of repentance.

Our Father in heaven took His anger out on Jesus Christ so that we could be in fellowship with Him. God will never break His covenant with His Son or with us. Our heavenly Father's heart is only for our good and training us in holiness. He wants us to learn to live as He is: holy, righteous, pure, and living in the eternal realm of heaven and prosperity. He trains us to be like Him. His gracious training and discipline are stated in Hebrews.

> And have you completely forgotten this word of encouragement that addresses you as a father addresses his son? It says, "My son, do not make light of the Lord's discipline, and do not lose heart when he rebukes you, because the Lord disciplines the one he loves, and he chastens everyone he accepts as his son."
>
> Endure hardship as discipline; God is treating you as his children. For what children are not disciplined by their father? If you are not disciplined—and everyone

undergoes discipline—then you are not legitimate, not true sons and daughters at all. Moreover, we have all had human fathers who disciplined us and we respected them for it. How much more should we submit to the Father of spirits and live! They disciplined us for a little while as they thought best; but God disciplines us for our good, in order that we may share in his holiness. No discipline seems pleasant at the time, but painful. Later on, however, it produces a harvest of righteousness and peace for those who have been trained by it.

—HEBREWS 12:5–11, NIV

Jesus' death, resurrection, and ascension guarantee that we have a way back to the Father. We must believe in His love more than our sin, error, or mistakes. This is the essence of the ascension life. This is what God was trying to say through the whole process of Jesus' death, burial, and resurrection. Jesus said to Mary, "Listen, don't touch Me. I must go to the Father. You get to receive the Holy Spirit. In going to the Father, I get to be with the One who has carried Me through all this." We need to be those kinds of people. We need to be saying, "You know what? I will go to my Father, whom I love the most. And because I love Him the most, I can then love you." Those are statements of people who live in the heavenly seat of ascension and the prosperity realm.

In Jesus' parable, when the son confesses, the father says to the servants,

"Quick! Bring the best robe and put it on him. Put a ring on his finger and sandals on his feet. Bring the fattened calf and kill it. Let's have a feast and celebrate. For this son of mine was dead and is alive again; he was lost and is found." So, they began to celebrate.

—Luke 15:22–24, NIV

Celebration is a lifestyle of the heavenly seat of ascension and the eternal realm of prosperity. Heaven is prosperous and celebrates us and the victories that manifest in the earthly realm. Heaven celebrates when we act prosperously and when we respond victoriously in all circumstances.

In Luke 15, the Father was not just saying that you get these blessings. He was saying, "I'm giving you back everything you ran away from. You won't need to work harder, study more, or perform more. You can have the same position you had the day you ran out of here." He squandered everything, yet God's grace and mercy far outweigh anything we can imagine. That same Father loves you amid any of your circumstances or trials.

If you want to live the ascension life, you must learn for yourself the love of the Father. When you have His heart, you have His ways, which are prosperous. In Jesus' parable, the father's treatment of his prodigal son was as if no sin had ever occurred. God treats us, His prodigal children, as if eternity had the first say and the final death, burial, and resurrection of Jesus was enough. That young man had reentered the eternal realm, and all he had done was seen only from a heavenly perspective. In later chapters you will learn more about the eternal realm and the keys to living in these spaces for healing in your life.

You may not know your earthly father or your heavenly Father God the way I shared from Scripture. I know how much He loves you because He sent Jesus to die for your sins, mistakes, shame, and issues so that you could be raised to newness of life and enter the eternal portal of prosperity in His name. I saw the eternal realm of prosperity when I visited heaven and saw the Royal Table. You can read about my encounters with heaven in my book *Releasing Heaven*.[2]

Jesus spoke of this realm to His disciples.

> You are those who have stood by me in my trials. And I confer on you a kingdom, just as my Father conferred one on me, so that you may eat and drink at my table in my kingdom and sit on thrones, judging the twelve tribes of Israel.
>
> —Luke 22:28–30, niv

God has prepared a place for us, and it is a beautiful place. It's available to us today, even in the earthly realm. You receive that place by believing you are seated with Christ in heavenly places, far above all the warfare, issues, trials, and confusion, because God has raised you to be in that eternal place of prosperity. It is a realm of prosperous living where the soul is complete and whole. He gave us this place as a gift through Jesus, and now we can establish a relationship with the Father because His love makes us whole.

FAITH ACTIVATION

As an act of faith, please take an inventory of your relationship to the Father. As you are seated with Christ in ascension places, I know right now in the mighty name of Jesus that your relationship will begin to change even today. Open your heart to realize God's love for you. He causes all things to work together for your good, and He's prepared a place for you in the eternal realm of prosperity. You can go there even today in your prosperous mind by faith. Start this exercise by simply asking Him who He is. Ask Him about your relationship with Him. Share with Him who you are and what you believe or do not believe about Him. This is part of having a relationship with Him, and Jesus made the way. Just leap out in faith and begin talking to Him in prayer. Just share your heart no matter what is on it. That is the beginning. You can write these truths below and refer back to them later.

PRAYER OF FAITH

Father, we thank You so much for Your Word that raises us and shows us Your love. Thank You that You want us to live in this eternal realm of prosperity where we are ascended with You and know you personally as Father. Lord, right now, in the name of Jesus, release the seven spirits of the Lord—Your Spirit and the spirit of revelation, counsel, wisdom, understanding, might, and knowledge. Lord, help us open our Bibles so we can find the truth about who You are and establish a relationship with You in such a way that we manifest the glory of God. Amen.

QUESTIONS *for* REFLECTION

1. What kind of relationship do you have with your earthly father? What kind of relationship do you have with Father God?

2. Jesus secured your relationship with Father God through His death, resurrection, and ascension. What kind of relationship do you want to have with Father God? What changes do you need to make to facilitate this relationship with Father God?

3. What tools of prosperity from the Word of God will you begin to use so you can live your life in the prosperity realm?

CHAPTER 4

Kingdom Structure

THE WORD *PROSPERITY* means wholeness in the Bible. It means nothing missing and nothing broken in our souls, a shalom peace.[1] If you remember, in the preface I shared the truth about prosperity. We are called as kingdom citizens to live out the seat of ascension and the realm of prosperity in the earth. Jesus has given us an inheritance through His death, resurrection, and ascension that opens the power of this portal for everyday living. Let's continue learning about heavenly portals and the eternal realm of prosperity. Once your mind establishes the power of resting on things above, you will activate this dominion for kingdom living.

PROPHECY BUILDS THE HOUSE

Heavenly portals are doorways to a realm where we learn the foundations for living what Jesus called the abundant life on earth.

We can encounter the supernatural and live in a prosperous realm more frequently when we learn the structures of the eternal realm. In this chapter we will discuss the foundational pillars that build a life of prosperity—a life of shalom peace—where the eternal can impact the earthly and you can be a releaser of the glory on earth. If we want to live and rule with the authority of heaven, we need to build on the kingdom structures that bring forth the mind shifts we must have for prosperity in our souls. Prosperity of soul leads to being a releaser of the glory.

Our kingdom rulership is a permanent position and power that facilitates a life of hope, faith, and the glory of the Lord. We propel the Word of God prophetically, speaking into the dead places we face on earth. When the Word is spoken, life will come to dead things and prosperity will grow. This will birth a realm of prosperity where you can function daily. I want you to live prosperously because then you will have the most significant impact on the world around you.

If you live prosperously, you activate the eternal realm in foundational places where you need to release the glory. Building a kingdom structure is much like building a home. It's also how God builds our physical bodies and His church body. He starts with the bones first. The bones are the central framework that gives the body form and holds it together. The bones hold the temple in place and are the pillars of the flesh and sinew.

Ezekiel's vision of dry bones is a picture of how God builds His body and what is needed daily to be prosperous and carry out His plans on earth. Only the Word of God and the fire of His voice can do it. I will highlight scriptures in this chapter that will cause you to see things as God sees them so you can be prosperous in the earthly realm, which is God's will. He sent His Son Jesus so prosperity could reign on earth, because the eternal realm and prosperity was God's original plan in the Garden of Eden.

God has a burden for His church because His church is His body, the people He loves. The Lord told me that the bones of His church have become dry and brittle. He said, "They're starting to shake, and they're starting to crack." Our God is life-giving, and when He shows us things about His body, the church, He teaches us what we can do to strengthen the bone structure.

HEALING THE BONES

You probably know that low bone density increases the risk of developing osteoporosis. To increase our calcium, which helps prevent osteoporosis, we're told to eat green leafy vegetables and drink lots of milk. We are told to get lots of calcium from a young age so that when we grow older our bones will not become brittle.

I have a friend who is a healing evangelist, and she was diagnosed with bone cancer. She said the Lord gave her one scripture: "A cheerful heart is good medicine, but a crushed spirit dries up the bones" (Prov. 17:22, NIV). The King James Version puts it this way: "A merry heart doeth good like a medicine: but a broken spirit drieth the bones." She took that one scripture and spoke it over and over, and she practiced laughing. When the doctors told her she would die, she just laughed as she spoke this scripture to herself. She was entirely healed of bone cancer. Now she travels the world preaching the gospel and healing.

I have seen this scripture in action with multiple people as I minister healing. When people want to be set free from sickness in their bodies or minds, I often share this scripture. Most diseases are carried in the bones and cells of the depressed and downtrodden, so this scripture is uniquely effective.

The enemy wants to overwhelm God's children by putting burdens on them and telling them they are missing something, they are broken, and they can't be fixed. What a lie! This trick started with the serpent in the Garden of Eden, and Satan is still doing it today. He tries to put the spirit of death on us by getting us to accept that we are broken and cannot be fixed. Proverbs 17:22 is a great way to combat that spirit of death. It is prosperous to laugh in the face of death or the enemy. When we respond as though we are saved, healed, redeemed, and not broken, the enemy knows we have tapped into the power of life!

The Lord is concerned about His body because we are connected to the head, Jesus. We are *individuals* made in His image, but we are also a *body of believers* made in His image. Genesis 1:27 says, "So God created man in his own image, in the image of God created he him; male and female created he them." Adam and Eve were created in the image of God, and we are their descendants. First, the Lord brought forth Adam out of the earth. Genesis 3:19 says, "For dust thou art, and unto dust shalt thou return." Then God made Eve from the rib of Adam.

> And the LORD God caused a deep sleep to fall upon Adam, and he slept: and he took one of his ribs, and closed up the flesh instead thereof; And the rib, which the LORD God had taken from man, made he a woman, and brought her unto the man. And Adam said, This is now bone of my bones, and flesh of my flesh: she shall be called Woman, because she was taken out of Man.
>
> —GENESIS 2:21–23

Eve came from bone yanked out of the rib of Adam. The apostle Paul tells us in Ephesians 5:23 that the woman's head is the husband, and the wife is called to submit to the husband. In doing so, the husband is to love the wife just as Christ loved the church and washed her clean with the water of the Word. (See Ephesians 5:22–26.) The Word then says in Ephesians 5:30, "For we are members of his body, of his flesh, and of his bones." The apostle Paul says in Ephesians 5:32, "This is a great mystery: but I speak concerning Christ and the church." Paul brought forth this revelation to the Ephesian church from the understanding of men and women, but he was really speaking about Christ being the head of the church, and we the church being the body of Christ. Christ is the example of how husbands are to treat their wives, and women must reverence their husbands just as the body of Christ must be in reverence to our head, Jesus.

If what you just read wasn't enough truth, here are some more godly truths about men and women in the body of Christ. The wife is considered to be the glory or glow of the husband. She's to come forth as being the one who is reflecting the love that's between the husband and the wife. Paul says, "Man is the image and glory of God: but the woman is the glory of the man" (1 Cor. 11:7, NIV). Women glow differently than men, but the apostle Paul tells us we are both important to the body and members of His church.

In *The Message*, Proverbs 3:8 says, "Your body will glow with health, your very bones will vibrate with life!" When your body glows life is being projected out of it. A healthy body shines with life and brings forth the glory of the Lord in the earthly realm. A body whose bones are healthy and strong glows with the eternal life of Christ and represents the glow of life in the earthly realm. A body like this is living in the heavenly eternal realm, which is being manifest on earth.

PROPER ALIGNMENT

A glowing body is in alignment with the head. That is why it is glowing. But what happens when people have broken bones? Their skeletal system is now out of alignment. If your bone breaks, you must go in for an alignment to get it set properly to move with the rest of the body. Otherwise there will be a tremendous amount of pain, and that particular part of your body will not be functioning well. The same thing is true for back, hip, or neck issues. Often a chiropractor must put the spine back into alignment and reduce pressure on the bone structure.

Fivefold ministry leaders—apostles, prophets, pastors, teachers, and evangelists—are all called to equip or perfect the body. (See Ephesians 4:11–16.) They are called to help mend the broken bones and align them with the head, Jesus Christ. The Greek word for *equipping* or *perfecting* is *katartismos*, which is broken down to *katartizo* and means to completely or thoroughly repair, adjust, fit, frame, mend, restore, and join.[2] This is what is needed to fix a broken bone. This mending brings us from a place of brokenness as individuals and as a body through one head, Jesus Christ, who gave His life so that we no longer have anything missing or broken.

Why is this so important? The Bible says we are tossed to and fro by the enemy's lies because we are broken individuals with broken souls (mind, will, and emotions) who hear all kinds of voices and don't know what to do. We are easily deceived. We get back into alignment when the spoken word of truth is given to us in love. Then we can grow up into Jesus, who is our head. This happens when the church moves from a mindset of poverty and brokenness to one of prosperity of soul and victorious ascension. It's when we know we are seated with Christ in heavenly places, and now we are open in faith to invite the prosperity realm to impact our earthly realm.

This lines up with 3 John 2, which says, "Beloved, I wish above all things that thou mayest prosper and be in health, even as thy soul prospereth." This is the essence of prosperous living. When our souls are no longer broken but mended in faith in every area, then we have adopted our inheritance as ones ascended with Christ and seated with Him. Here we are in proper alignment with our head, Jesus Christ, and even seated with Him in royalty as heirs of the King. We are now called to rule as kingdom citizens with nothing missing or broken. We are now protected from the enemy, who seeks to devour those who are broken. We are mended by the word of truth and the redemption of our souls and bodies because of Jesus' shed blood, resurrection, and ascension.

PROPHECY REVEALED

Earlier in this chapter I shared what the Lord spoke to me about the church's bones shaking and being out of alignment. The Lord told me, "I need them to come back into alignment with Me, the head, the King of the universe. I need them to check their hearts and stop aligning with everything they're seeing." In other words, God said the church is being tossed to and fro because of brokenness in the body of Christ.

Do you realize that when evil things or wrong things are called good, it gives cancer to your bones and they will become brittle? When this happens you must get back into alignment. Learn to exercise and eat right. Stick to that New Year's resolution you made, or turn over a new leaf no matter what time of year it is. If you've taken in too much of what's not good, you need to overhaul your life.

It is the same with the body of Christ. The Lord says, "My church has been eating too much of what's not good. And the foods they're eating, the words they're saying, and the things they're propagating are not producing the result I want to see on earth." He says, "When I came, the kingdom of heaven arrived."

The church of Jesus Christ is to be apostolic, which means we are sent ones, commissioned to infiltrate areas on behalf of the government that sends us. Who is the head of government in the heavenly realm, or the kingdom of our God? It is Jesus Christ. He is the head of government in the kingdom of heaven. When He speaks, those who've received Jesus as their Lord and Savior are to come into alignment with Him and see, hear, and say everything as He does.

When countries are conquered, government officials establish that country under the new sovereign leader. This takes place in the earthly realm. For example, every time Great Britain conquered a nation, that nation became subject to whatever Britain's sovereign king or queen said. The British monarch became the ruler of that newly acquired kingdom, and that nation was now under their sovereign dominion. This is how earthly governments were run in the past, and some still are in the present. When sovereigns dictate orders, their subjects follow through.

This concept is a biblical one. Our sovereign, King Jesus, has dictated the way He wants things. But currently He says His church needs to listen better to His voice. The Lord says, "My church is listening to many other voices but is not listening to Me."

He knows His body is made up of humans, frail creatures that He had to die, resurrect, and ascend for. However, He has given us every reason and made available every power to do what He says; we are just not doing it. We cannot continue to make excuses for our frailty or consider ourselves victims. We must right, exercise, and make some changes." Why would someone say that? Because they want to live.

Spiritually speaking, I know you want to live. You bought this book to read a life-giving word that will cause you to keep breathing life every day and doing what the Father says. Hopefully, you gather for fellowship with other members of the body and speak life to them and invite the Holy Spirit to minister to them. This is how the members of the body regain their strength and become a part of the global work that the sovereign ruler is doing.

The apostolic church needs to know that it's been called to make disciples of all nations. However, God says, "Together we not make disciples of all nations if you don't speak the way I want you to speak." The apostles went forth with a word that was pure and unadulterated from the King. As the apostolic church our job is to speak what's true even when the truth is alarming and us.

This has been going on since the beginning of time. There's always been people. There's always been a remnant. We can follow in footsteps of devoted followers of Jesus Christ who have gone before us and say, "We don't have to do it that way. We can speak love. We can speak righteousness. We can speak peace. We will be the carriers of the word of God.

We lean on ourselves to be followers of the King. You through hearing and reading the Word of God, in action when you know Him and have Him.

But what's evil and what's good, please of God. I believe the Lord is saying, "I Word, digesting it every day so I can

stand up and do what our sovereign ruler says. The problem is that we often don't know what Jesus is saying because we have too many other voices continually speaking to us.

To rule as citizens of the eternal kingdom that He is sovereign ruler over, we must know from the Word of God, having our souls cleansed, that we are no longer broken but fixed and made whole. We must rule by saying what He says and doing what He does to change ungodly environments.

This is nothing new. This is the story of the gospel. When Jesus walked the earth He said, "The kingdom of heaven is here, and you must do what I do" (paraphrased). His words and actions went totally against what the earthly government wanted Him to do, which is why Isaiah prophesied that the government would be on His shoulders (Isa. 9:6). This is also why He was crucified at the hands of the government.

We know there is corruption in government of any kind, anywhere, anyplace on earth. But here's another truth: when you know Jesus Christ as your Lord and Savior, you are called to abide by the just, truthful, uncorrupt heavenly government and develop that kingdom structure and way of doing things on earth.

God is asking us to speak and stand for the eternal heavenly realm. We are called to speak the Word of God and do exactly what our sovereign ruler wants us to do. We are kingdom citizens under Jesus' rulership first. God wants to strengthen us to live like our governmental head, Jesus. Here's what I believe He is saying to us now:

> I want My church to be strengthened. My body cannot respond weakly. If I am not weak, My body cannot respond that way, as I am not that way. If the head moves to the right, the body's got to turn to the right; if the head

moves to the left, the body's got to turn as well. Otherwise you will be out of alignment.

I want my people to remember kingdom structure first. I want them to remember the kingdom above all things. And then I will put in order the things of the earth. But if they don't understand the kingdom first and are confused by what's happening on earth, they will not speak what I want them to say. They will not see the way I want them to see.

GOD'S GARDEN KINGDOM

How will we do this? How will we fix this problem? We must fix the problem by knowing and understanding God's command to Adam and Eve in Genesis chapter 1.

> Be fruitful, and multiply, and replenish the earth, and subdue it: and have dominion over the fish of the sea, and over the fowl of the air, and over every living thing that moveth upon earth.
>
> —Genesis 1:28

In addition, we need to remember that when Jesus died, resurrected, and ascended, the church also ascended with Him. This is now our positional authority on earth as kingdom citizens with kingdom rulership. Everything flows from this realm of prosperity now.

When Adam and Eve ate the forbidden fruit, Satan stole this power from the children of the Most High, who were made in the very image of God. Satan is a thief. If a thief comes to your house, will you fight to keep that thief out? Or will you let him come in and ravage everything?

When the body of Christ allows every voice and sight to come in and influence it, it's saying, Bring that thief in and let

him have his way. The church has been given a mandate, a we need to examine whether we are following through wit If something is not fruitful, multiplying, increasing, or r ishing itself, if you aren't able to subdue it, and you car dominion over it, you'd better ask yourself whether it's

In this world we do not hear voices telling us to b to increase, multiply, subdue, replenish, or have dor usually hear such things as, "Hide, suffocate, be bur Those instructions are not life; they are death.

The Word of God says the kingdom of heaven are to be government agents of the sovereign K this way:

> The time is fulfilled, and the kingdom of
> repent ye, and believe the gospel.

Jesus has come and fulfilled the wh death, and the grave. The apostolic ch kingdom of heaven on earth. The r of the kingdom of God. The world different now—that sin is not si believe this, we allow toxins to

In your physical body toxin notice. If you aren't paying a toxins enter your body. It s might even become aware "Well, this is how I'm liv since I'm already full mean, what's the diff say, "No more toxi keep them healthy, strong, and whole. Then I need them to take that Word that is changing and transforming them and project it into an area that is not doing that very thing. I'm calling them to change the lack and poverty environments into prosperous environments of the kingdom." The Word of God opens portals or doorways to the eternal realm of prosperity where God's kingdom citizens gain the power to rule and reign on earth.

I hope you understand that God wants to put His kingdom structure back in order. The Word of God reveals God's order for the earth. It contains directives on what needs to take place in the earthly realm, and we are the recipients of that direction. The job of apostles, prophets, pastors, teachers, and evangelists is to equip the body, *katartismos,* by aligning worldly kingdoms with what God is saying in the here and now.

DRY BONES COME TO LIFE

The prophet Ezekiel can teach us keys that open heavenly portals and enable us to rule as kingdom citizens. In Ezekiel 37, God was viewing the earth and wanted to make a change. He asked His prophet to start operating even when Ezekiel had trouble seeing with spiritual eyes.

This is a lesson about heavenly portals. Sometimes prophets don't see well initially, but by faith they can access the heavenly realm when sight in the spirit begins to function. Sometimes God has to prompt the seer to see in the spiritual realm by saying, "Tell Me what you see." In other words, God is saying, "I, the Lord, want to do something, prophet, so build your faith. Have the faith of God, prophet, and tell Me what you see."

This is also how God's prophetic church works, as we are a prophetic people as His kingdom body. God wants to know what you see in a situation, whether natural sight into the earth realm or spiritual sight into the spirit realm. *He is expecting that you will see prosperously because you know His heart and who He is.* If you see poverty and lack, then He knows you are not seeing like Him. In such cases He will prompt you to see like Him.

Check out this dialogue as God prompts Ezekiel to see like Him.

> The hand of the LORD was upon me, and carried me out in the spirit of the LORD, and set me down in the midst of the valley which was full of bones, and caused me to pass by them round about: and, behold, there were very many in the open valley; and, lo, they were very dry. And he said unto me, Son of man, can these bones live? And I answered, O Lord GOD, thou knowest.
>
> —EZEKIEL 37:1–3

God asks, "Can these bones live?" That word *live* in Hebrew means to revive, recover, repair, or give promise.[3] God is saying, "Can these bones, which are structure, substance, and foundation for the body, come alive?" God is beckoning the prophet to see as He sees.

The prophet answers, "I don't know, but You know, Lord." He's saying, "You are the giver of life. I can't see what You see from this mess in the earthly realm, but I want to meet You where You are, Lord." The word *knowest* in Hebrew means to ascertain by seeing correctly.[4] God properly ascertains what He sees, and we can too when we understand how to stay in the heavenly eternal realm flowing with prosperity, which is an abundance of life.

I can tell you, as a person who moves in the prophetic, that I can't "see" until I tap into the faith of God for something—then I can see what He sees. Things in the natural or earthly realm may look dark, dismal, and full of sin and destruction. Earthly things usually look like this because of the attack of Satan in the garden. Our natural eyes always see these things first, and then we see hope later. We are more prone in our flesh to see negativity and darkness. We must be prompted from a heavenly position of faith to see as God sees and bring that word to the earth to change it.

When God says to Ezekiel, "This is what I see," things begin to change and reflect the heavenly realm of prosperity. God always sees things the way they are with no deception. We see deception from the earthly realm, but not God. He sees from His realm of heaven and prosperity. When we align with how God sees, we are functioning in the heavenly realm of prosperity. This will cause miracles to happen, and life will come to the dead things.

Let's read what happens next with Ezekiel.

> Again he said unto me, Prophesy upon these bones, and say unto them, O ye dry bones, hear the word of the LORD. Thus saith the LORD God unto these bones; Behold, I will cause breath to enter into you, and ye shall live: And I will lay sinews upon you, and will bring up flesh upon you, and cover you with skin, and put breath in you, and ye shall live; and ye shall know that I am the LORD. So I prophesied as I was commanded: and as I prophesied, there was a noise, and behold a shaking, and the bones came together, bone to his bone. And when I beheld, lo, the sinews and the flesh came up upon them, and the skin covered them above: but there was no breath in them. Then said he unto me, Prophesy unto the wind, prophesy, son of man, and say to the wind, Thus saith the LORD God; Come from the four winds, O breath, and breathe upon these slain, that

they may live. So I prophesied as he commanded me, and the breath came into them, and they lived, and stood up upon their feet, an exceeding great army.

—EZEKIEL 37:4–10

Let's break this down. The Hebrew for *dry* is *yabesh*, which means ashamed, confused, disappointed as in failing, dry up as in water, wither as in plants, confounded, or shamed.[5] When God says to tell the dry bones to hear the word of the Lord, He is saying, "You who are in dry places, you who are ashamed, confused, disappointed, and you who are in a place of death will now come alive!" God's heart is for us to come alive in every way.

He says to prophesy, which is *naba* in Hebrew and means to speak or sing by inspiration.[6] He sings over us as the Bible tells us: "The LORD thy God in the midst of thee is mighty; he will save, he will rejoice over thee with joy; he will rest in his love, he will joy over thee with singing" (Zeph. 3:17). This singing by inspiration and joy is part of who He is in His eternal realm of prosperity, and this realm will impact flesh and sinew.

Picture it this way: there are dead bones in the valley—no life whatsoever—but the life-giver Himself speaks to the prophet and says, "Let's do this together. I want you to speak. And then as you speak My heart of prosperity, and as you prophesy from this realm of heaven where I see, I will do what only I can do." *He wanted Ezekiel, a human who had authority given to him like Adam did in the garden, to participate with Him to bring life into the earth. He wanted to be one with Ezekiel in the speaking.*

Ezekiel's prophecy also was a prophecy of unity to come through Jesus, who brought fulfillment and alignment with heaven. We prophesy today from fulfillment and oneness with God having taken place. Jesus overcame sin, death, and the grave. Jesus is now resurrected, seated in the heavenlies, and we are seated with Him. We now have that fullness, that power of dominion of life, anytime we want to speak prophetically to the dry bones of our lives and nations. We have adopted the life-giving capacity of the life-giver, Jesus, when we position ourselves from the eternal realm. It is from this identity we speak.

SPEAK LIFE

When you prophesy, you speak the word God gives you, and then God has to come and meet the word that was spoken. Similar to Ezekiel, the prophet Jeremiah was also trained by God to see as He sees and then speak it.

> Moreover the word of the LORD came unto me, saying, Jeremiah, what seest thou? And I said, I see a rod of an almond tree. Then said the LORD unto me, Thou hast well seen: for I will hasten my word to perform it.
>
> —JEREMIAH 1:11–12

When we speak a word from God's realm of sight, which is the seat of ascension and the eternal realm of prosperity, He then comes to perform it. Therefore, when we speak a prophetic word, something is happening. Life is being emitted into the earth.

How many times have you been prompted to speak a prophetic word in a moment, but you held your tongue for fear of how someone might perceive the view you have and be offended? Maybe God wanted to make a prosperous move in that very place. The enemy wants to stop prosperous moves of God because he knows the power of life and death are in the tongue, and if death can keep its hold, then Satan can continue to work in the earthly realm in that place.

You might think, "They won't believe what I say, and they won't grab hold of this, so I will not talk. I am afraid of offending even with my positive comments of what I see God doing." You don't make the results. All you're called to do is speak to the dry bones and get them in alignment with life-giving power.

If we go back to Ezekiel 37, the next thing the Lord told Ezekiel was to prophesy to the wind. That means he was told to speak life so it would come into that place. That's the breath of God. The Lord said,

> Prophesy unto the wind, prophesy, son of man, and say to the wind, Thus saith the Lord God; Come from the four winds, O breath, and breathe upon these slain, that they may live. So I prophesied as he commanded me, and the breath came into them, and they lived, and stood up upon their feet, an exceeding great army.
>
> —EZEKIEL 37:9–10

In Hebrew, this word *breath* is *ruach*, which is wind or spirit.[7] Not only do we, the body of Christ, prophesy the word of God, but as kingdom citizens we are to call the breath of God, the Holy Spirit, the *ruach*, to be activated in our lives and situations. God tells Ezekiel to consult the four winds. The four winds of breath are Holy Spirit power from the north, south, east, and west, where the Spirit flows from all four corners of the earth. Prayer that activates this power churns up the earth and makes it spin forth, just like a tornado pulling everything together. That's a portal opening where life comes down on what is dead and makes it come alive. The four corners gather in a breath of His life from heaven, making it a portal of heaven on earth.

PRACTICAL PROPHETIC PORTALS

Let me make this practical for you. We are called as kingdom citizens seated with Christ in heavenly places to stir up the breath of God from the four winds and speak life into the dry, confused places of the earthly realm. These dry places include your home, neighborhood, city, state, nation, and nations. Start with your family. Prophesy to the dry, unliving thing that looks dead in your marriage. Prophesy to your child or grandchild who's living in dryness or not fulfilling their destiny. Prophesy to your infant, whom you want to see fulfilling his or her destiny and being raised in a holy nation. You have God's life-giving power to change your environment by prophesying, speaking life, and asking the Holy Spirit to come and breathe on anything not moving.

Next in the long dialogue in Ezekiel 37, God begins to speak to the nation of Israel in verses 11–14. Positionally in the present, you can apply this to God speaking to the nation you live in. God says to Ezekiel that the people have declared that their bones are dried up, their hope is gone, they are cut off. That's what Israel felt during this time, and it's what you may feel about your nation now. You may feel your own heart is dried up, hope is gone, and you are cut off. Maybe you feel your home is dried up, your church is dried up, your nation is dried up, and you are not in your land, but you are in bondage in someone else's land.

Stop, I say! You are spinning out of control with lies and death. What do you see? Open your eyes! Look again and see the living God positioning us all as seated kings and rulers of nations. Step in and prophesy to what is dead and make it come alive. That is God's will, and He will perform His word.

This is very, very important: We are not dead. We are not cut off. We are not without hope.

ALIGNMENT WITH THE FATHER

We must be in one accord, in unity, and begin to speak life to dead places. Remember, the prosperity realm comes through the portal of life and is made possible by Jesus' death, resurrection, and ascension. That's the truth. We as the body are called to lead the earth in the direction the Lord desires for His return. We do have hope. We are not cut off from our Savior, Jesus. He does rule. He does reign. We are part of the kingdom. We have a responsibility to prophesy and to pray to all dead environments in Jesus' name.

In Ezekiel 37:12, the Word says, "Thus saith the Lord God; Behold, O my people, I will open your graves, and cause you to come up out of your graves, and bring you into the land of Israel." Today this means that God brought us back to Him when Jesus died, resurrected, and ascended. We go to a deeper understanding of this as we actively tap into the heavenly realm that brings the heart of the Father into our hearts, homes, neighborhoods, and nations through repentance and confession. These blessings are already ours because of the resurrection and ascension, but we must activate what is ours by faith, by seeing things as Jesus does. Kingdom structure is about entering the heavenly realm to release God's glory on earth.

Then the Lord told Ezekiel,

> The word of the LORD came again unto me, saying, Moreover, thou son of man, take thee one stick, and write upon it, For Judah, and for the children of Israel his companions: then take another stick, and write upon it, For

Joseph, the stick of Ephraim and for all the house of Israel his companions: And join them one to another into one stick; and they shall become one in thine hand.
—EZEKIEL 37:15–17

In other words, God is saying, "Whatever has been divided will now become one." When the body of Christ is not in alignment, it causes division, which creates confusion. Whatever is dry creates confusion and division, but whatever is brought together as one family can stand.

In verses 21–27, God tells Ezekiel (and I'm paraphrasing): "I will make them one nation in the land, on the mountains of Israel. There will be one King over all of them, and they will never again be two nations or divided into two kingdoms. They will no longer defile themselves with their idols and vile images or with any of their offenses for I will save them from all their sinful backsliding, and I will cleanse them. They will be My people, and I will be their God. Jesus is from the line of King David, so this is God calling all nations unto Himself in Jesus under the one true living God. Two scriptures that share this truth are:

The LORD hath sworn in truth unto David; he will not turn from it; of the fruit of thy body will I set upon thy throne.
—PSALM 132:11

I have made a covenant with my chosen, I have sworn unto David my servant, Thy seed will I establish for ever, and build up thy throne to all generations. Selah.
—PSALM 89:3–4

It's interesting how the Lord tells Ezekiel the two nations will become one: when they get rid of all their graven images, their sin, and the various things representing death that they think are OK. The Bible says, "Woe unto them that call evil good, and good evil; that put darkness for light, and light for darkness; that put bitter for sweet, and sweet for bitter!" (Isa. 5:20). When people think that evil is good, it's dangerous. Some things are wrong because they don't match up with the Father and who He is. We can't redefine them as good just because that's the way our culture wants us to see them.

We are created in the image of God. Therefore we should only do what our Father is doing and see what our Father is seeing. God is life, and our image is life. It is hard to prophesy if we see evil as good because that means we see with earthly eyes. Yet we are called to prophesy from eternal life, a sacred space in heavenly places. You don't prophesy what you see from an earth perspective because that has no power. You are just telling what is going on in the natural, present moment, which is dead anyway. It's not what God sees.

Ask God right now to purify you so that you can see as He sees, which will be a view from holiness, righteousness, and life. Repent of any known areas of sin and ask Him for forgiveness. Ask Him to show you from a heavenly perspective what He sees about your situation. We often can't see as He sees until we cleanse ourselves of impurities and sin.

HOLINESS OPENS PORTALS

Kingdom structure is getting into alignment with the Father. This is about our relationship with our Dad. We are the children of the King, and therefore we must act like the King. God says He will unite divided and broken kingdoms when they agree to give up vile images and sinful ways and choose to fight for justice, righteousness, and peace. These are things that the

Father holds dear to the point that He sacrificed His precious Son, Jesus Christ, to redeem us.

> Follow peace with all men, and holiness, without which no man shall see the Lord:
>
> —HEBREWS 12:14

When David committed adultery with Bathsheba, he acknowledged his sin in Psalm 51:1–4. When we come to realize our personal choices are less about us and more about what we believe to be true about Him, we begin to assess our thoughts so we will not do certain things. Our sinful nature because of the fall of man is prone to disregard authority and have no honor. Therefore, when we think about bowing to our sovereign King, we can't even understand that concept because we have disavowed so much authority along the way.

But there is good news: God made a way so that we would not be dried up. When we realize we have not lost hope and we are not cut off, that's the good news. When we speak to the dead things in our lives from understanding our place of ascension as His kingdom rulers, that place of identity in Him, we will see the manifest presence and power of God. Jesus and the Holy Spirit are our guarantee of this.

As a body in alignment with the head, Jesus, the church can say in unity, "God will come through." He is living, active, and present, and He wants to bring life to your situation. All you have to do is prophesy, speak by the Holy Spirit to the Holy Spirit, and you will see the results come to pass. If God could breathe life into bones with no flesh, tendons, and ligaments in the valley of dry bones, if He could breathe life into the dust of the earth and create Adam, He can do it now.

Remember: We are not dried up. We are not cut off. We are not without hope. He is our living God who still ministers even today, and He does so through *you and me*. We are the church. We're His hands. We're His feet. We are all He has right now. We must not allow the devil to create division. Yes, it's true. Sin has to be called forth for what it is because there's no sin in Him. We can't call what is evil good.

We must know and understand that our job as the church of Jesus Christ is to become the voice of God. Many times in the Word of God, the word *voice* is broken down to be the Hebrew word *qol*, which means spark or fire.[8] When the voice of the Lord comes, it produces a spark or a fire that then begins to move. And as the fire begins to move, change happens. When fire touches something, everything changes.

PRAYER FOR PORTAL OF LIFE

I encourage you to pray along with this prayer and humbly speak to the Lord.

> We thank You, Lord, that You love us and that we are the bones of Your body. We speak life to our very bones, Father, and life to any bones around us that may be dead and lifeless. We speak life to decaying bones, Lord, and we ask You to revive those bones. We ask You to send the Holy Spirit's presence to breathe on those bones and bring them life.
>
> We call forth the four winds of Your Spirit from the north, south, east, and west, Father. We want to be Your church with nothing missing and nothing broken, standing in complete alignment with You. We know

that's where life-giving power comes from. We thank You, Jesus, for life-giving power.

Lord Jesus, I speak faith right now to the people, to the nations, to have the faith of God. Lord, the prophet Ezekiel had to believe in You and what You told him. God, we believe for families right now to be restored. We believe for broken marriages to be put back into place. We believe for new organs and strength to broken bodies and broken bones. Lord Jesus, put broken places back together right now, and where members have gone astray, bring them home. Lord, we call them back in the name of Jesus. They will come back to You, Father, and they will repent and receive forgiveness. We pray that anything we worship or hold higher than You, Lord, shall be torn down. You should be put on the throne in our homes and hearts. Lord, You made a way through Jesus Christ, the new covenant, who was cut in His flesh so that now new life would come forth. We ask You to cut out every dead thing in our lives and bring forth new life to those places that remain, and we thank You for raising us to be seated with Christ in heavenly places. We thank You, Father.

FAITH ACTIVATIONS

In an act of faith, please receive the life-giving power right now, anywhere you may feel dead in your body, anywhere that God might be giving you a thought of what needs to change. Anything that looks dead, I want you to speak to it, saying, "It's not cut off. It's not dry. It is not without hope. It is not without faith."

If you have not yet confessed Jesus as your Lord and Savior

or want to begin to confess places that are hurting, broken, or missing—or sin—in your life, do it now. This chapter has been about celebrating the redemption that King Jesus bought for us. He sent His Son Jesus to die on the cross and be buried. He shed His blood for the forgiveness of sins. We're no longer cut off because we are forgiven by His blood. All you need to do is confess that you are a sinner and you believe Jesus died for your sin. Then simply ask for forgiveness. We've all fallen short. Not one of us has done only right. We have all done wrong. We all need to humbly repent and thank God for what His Son, Jesus, did for us. You are not cut off if you prayed this in agreement and just spoke it out to the Lord.

TAKE COMMUNION

Let's take communion together. Wherever you are reading this, find any type of bread or cracker and some grape juice (or anything to drink) and then sit and think about His sacrifice for you. Communion says that we are not divided, but we are one. We are one body, one flesh, the Lord, Jesus Christ. His shed blood and His broken body on the cross unite us as one—no matter our backgrounds, our histories, the differences or diversities that lie between us. When we forsake sin and receive Him, we become one. We stand before Him as one unified through His broken body and shed blood. When we receive communion, we receive it because we have been healed, saved, redeemed, and made whole by the blood of Jesus. We are forgiven. We are not cut off. We are not dried up but are living, breathing, created in the image of the Lord, and connected to the Father. Take communion wherever you are right now by eating that bread and thanking Him for His body that was broken for you. Then drink the juice as a reminder that He shed His blood for you. Now thank Him!

QUESTIONS *for* REFLECTION

1. What areas in your life did you identify as dried up and broken? Confess below your healing in those areas after praying and taking communion.

2. What fear have you overcome about prophesying now that you understand it as speaking life to dead places in your life and your environment?

3. How will you continue as a member of Christ's body to remain unified in your own house and the house of God?

CHAPTER 5

Portals in Times and Seasons

THE REALM OF the kingdom is ours when we fully align with the Father. As we read in the previous chapter, aligning ourselves with the truth of the Word of God, who we are, and where we are seated in heavenly places gives us the authority to access heavenly portals. These gateways open an eternal realm of prosperity in which we receive the resources of heaven that will change our earthly environments. We need to know how to walk in the authority and power He's given us in the kingdom realm. We learn more about the heavenly kingdom through encounters with that realm.

This chapter will share how to watch for the times, seasons, spaces, and places for heavenly portals. You will learn to participate with God by understanding the portals that enable you to encounter heaven and effect change on earth. I will show you what Scripture teaches about how to respond to these portals and receive from God through them. When heavenly portals are active, words of knowledge and words of wisdom flow quickly, and God meets the needs of His people. Whenever there are heavenly portals, there is healing. There are shifts. There is movement. Great things come from heaven. There are also financial blessings and miracles. These blessings suddenly show up because heavenly portals are gateways for the supernatural.

SEASONAL PORTALS

Let me start by sharing an encounter I had with the Lord during a particular season. I was in a semi-conscious dream state, and the Lord showed me an open heavenly portal and said, "I want you to speak on heavenly portals." The open portal I saw was huge, and the essence of God flowed through it. After I had this encounter, I looked on the Hebrew calendar to investigate historically when heavenly portals are the most active. I discovered that they are most active at the beginning of the Hebrew months and during the feasts or festivals of God, which happen seven times a year.

My semi-conscious dream encounter happened at the end of Hanukkah on the first day of Tevet in 2020, which is the tenth month on the Hebrew calendar and usually lines up with December–January of the Gregorian calendar. It is the fourth month on the civil calendar.

Each month on the Hebrew calendar begins with Rosh Chodesh, a day to celebrate the firstfruits of the month. Rosh Chodesh is either the first or second day of the month, depending on how many days are in the month. The Jewish people celebrate the first day or two in a month because a new month is a fresh start. This is why I believe that every time the month turns over, heavenly portals are more active.

At the beloved church that my husband and I founded, Freedom Destiny Church in Orange Park, Florida, we celebrated Rosh Chodesh each month of the Hebrew calendar year. We also celebrated the seven feasts of the Lord and special days on God's Hebrew calendar. During these special times on the calendar God did all kinds of things in the church body and in our hearts, and many miracles happened.

Every year, I look for the beginning of each month or Rosh Chodesh on the Hebrew calendar. I teach a course on this very subject called *Journey Through the Hebrew Calender* so you can know when each month begins and how to join with God to see the miracles of the season.[1]

My encounter with God happened during the Feast of Dedication, or Hanukkah, which is characterized in the winter season as a week of miracles. This celebration starts on the twenty-fifth day of the month of Kislev each year and lasts eight days. It is a time of remembering the miracle of the oil burning in the temple. In this courageous story, the Maccabees, a Jewish family that defended the temple, cleansed it, and rededicated it, found a vial of oil that was left after the temple's desecration, and this one vial miraculously burned in the menorah for eight days.

Hanukkah is a season where the miraculous is evident. At this same time of year Christians who follow the Gregorian calendar celebrate Christmas, a season of joy and celebration of the birth of the Messiah. Because the earthly realm has determined to celebrate the birth of the Messiah, as the earth rejoices it comes into a powerful agreement of faith with the heavenlies, which opens heavenly portals.

Remember, a heavenly portal is a door or gateway where there is no boundary between heaven and earth. It is a supernatural phenomenon where the expanse of the earth sky opens, and it's much easier to access heaven. We already access heaven because we're seated with Christ in heavenly places because of Jesus' death, resurrection, and ascension (Eph. 2:6). That gateway is available to us all the time. However, there are other times on the calendar when the earth and the realm of the first heaven (where our guardian angels and the fallen angels reside) and the second heaven (where demonic forces or fallen angels reside) are not interrupting what the third heaven is doing. The third heaven is where the Lord and heavenly hosts reside. No demonic forces reside there at all. It is the abode of God.

Sometimes heaven has to fight to impact the earth. How do we know this? In the Book of Daniel, Daniel prayed and fasted for twenty-one days before the archangel Michael came to answer his prayers (Dan. 1:12–14). Warfare happens in the first and second realms of heaven. Opposing forces are pushed back and not allowed to activate at their usual levels. But when portals are open, there are more accessible points on earth. It means that prayers are quickly answered and a response from heaven easily comes forth.

Portals are active during specific times and seasons such as the feasts of the Lord and other dates on the Hebrew calendar. Understanding this is a practical or natural way to know when we can expect to see moves of God on earth. When there are easier access times and seasons, this means the angelic hosts can travel faster to distribute the things that we need from heaven in the moment.

PORTALS IN HOLY EARTHLY PLACES

Portals are not only attributed to special times and seasons but also to specific places. When we talk about heavenly visitations coming through heavenly portals, we can also attribute that to being in a sanctuary in a church or dedicated place to the Lord. When you're in a sanctuary of the Lord and people are corporately worshipping and honoring the Lord, it opens a heavenly portal. Sometimes people refer to this as an "open heaven." Our worship creates easier access for the Holy Spirit's presence, angelic hosts, and miraculous encounters. Every church, anywhere, that worships the Lord is setting an environment of holiness.

There are other places on the planet that host open heavenly portals. One of those is the land of Israel. When you visit certain places in Israel, you feel no barrier between heaven and earth. One such place is Bethel, where God met Jacob and he saw angels ascending and descending (Gen. 28:10–22). Many sense the holiness of certain locations in Jerusalem, such as the Garden Tomb, where some theologians say Jesus was resurrected.

When you are in these places and begin to pray, you immediately sense that your prayer is answered. The friction from the first and second heaven is not causing interruptions. It's just incredible, and faith is high. There are no boundaries at all. It doesn't matter how you might personally feel about yourself or your environment in these portal places. In other words, heavenly portals will defy your negativity, doubts, and fears.

If you come into such a portal with any doubt, your doubt will dissolve as your faith supersedes it. If you come in with fear, the release of heaven into the earth will completely shatter that fear and how you feel about yourself, and you can hear and respond to what heaven is doing. These incredible experiences are available to us. The eternal heavenly realm carries no fear because in that realm the dominions of sin, death, and the grave are defeated. When this happens the eternal realm impacts the earthly realm with a glory release.

In Freedom Destiny we had one of these portals to the right of our altar. When we moved into our large building, we discovered that angels went up and down this portal all the time. People would praise the Lord in that corner continually because it was so filled with heaven. Again, open portals are based on times, seasons, and places.

DREAMS CAN OPEN PORTALS

Heavenly portals are also open in your dreams or semiconscious states where heaven can speak to you and give you answers. My testimony is an example of this. And according to Scripture, angelic activity takes place in our dreams. One example is in Matthew's account of the birth of Jesus.

> This is how the birth of Jesus the Messiah came about: His mother Mary was pledged to be married to Joseph, but before they came together, she was found to be pregnant through the Holy Spirit. Because Joseph her husband was faithful to the law, and yet did not want to expose her to public disgrace, he had in mind to divorce her quietly.
>
> But after he had considered this, an angel of the Lord appeared to him in a dream and said, "Joseph son of David, do not be afraid to take Mary home as your wife, because what is conceived in her is from the Holy Spirit. She will give birth to a son, and you are to give him the name Jesus, because he will save his people from their sins."
>
> All this took place to fulfill what the Lord had said through the prophet: "The virgin will conceive and give birth to a son, and they will call him Immanuel" (which means "God with us").
>
> When Joseph woke up, he did what the angel of the Lord had commanded him and took Mary home as his wife.

—Matthew 1:18–24, niv

Portals can be created in our dream states. In states of semi-consciousness we open ourselves to what heaven wants to say. This may or may not be of our own free will. In the above case of Joseph, it was not of his free will. He was determined to end his engagement to Mary. In other words, he believed in his heart, "She will not be my wife." But heaven accessed Joseph in a dream, and an angel was sent to him. This angel spoke heaven's desires to Joseph in such a way that when Joseph woke up from the dream, he knew he had encountered heaven, and he was able to make the right decision in that regard. The dream where heaven touched his heart caused him to alter his will.

Often the supernatural will speak to us in the night and the early morning hours when we are in semiconscious states because our flesh is not fighting during that time. Our flesh is able to receive. When heaven wants to invade a space, it does so when it has a relatively willing vessel: someone in a semiconscious state who's been resting and is more open to heavenly encounters.

The Bible calls Joseph a devout man. He and Mary were to be married. It was imperative to him that there be pureness and holiness in their marriage. That was in his heart already before the dream. In Joseph's case, the Lord had to intervene and speak to him so that he would be better positioned to do the will of God and not the law.

Joseph had a free will. He could have come out of the dream and still said, "I will not do what I saw. I will still divorce her." But that's not the kind of man he was. He knew that heaven had spoken to him through the encounter with an angel, and he knew that he had to decide. He had a free will, but he also had a heavenly encounter and instruction from the Lord. He had a choice to obey it.

When heaven meets us in our dreams and portals open, there is a purpose behind the portal. Sometimes an angel comes to us; other times we see pictures or scenes with people and places we may or may not be familiar with. These are insights into the direction the Lord wants us to go. When we wake up startled by what we've seen and felt in the experience, we know we've encountered heaven. We still decide whether we will follow and how we will respond. Nevertheless, heaven speaks to us through our dreams. They are portal passageways for heaven to come to earth.

ATTITUDES OF PROSPERITY OPEN PORTALS

The enemy wants you to think that everything about you is unholy, unrighteous, evil, and negative. This lie has been around since the days of Adam and Eve, who were told by the serpent that they were not who God said they were.

The more you saturate yourself with the Word of God, the more you defy the enemy's lies about you. You have great worth, and Jesus died and shed His blood so that you would be reconciled to Him. The more you build this foundational truth in your soul, the more you agree with God, and your soul will grow prosperous.

Once saved, you are called to a life of wholeness and purity. You are called to a life without guilt, condemnation, and the lies of the world. This heart attitude will open you to more heavenly encounters because you are aligning your life with what heaven says to be true about you. You enter by faith into prosperity and glory because Jesus made a way.

The more time you spend saturating your soul in God's Word,

the more you grow in knowledge and understanding of God's goodness and love for you. These soul changes transform you into the likeness of heaven, which removes the boundaries of unbelief, doubt, and fear in your soul. Jesus took care of the dominion of sin and death so there would be no boundary. Our boundary is ourselves and how we perceive ourselves based on what the world tells us. If you aim to understand what it means when you take on the identity of Christ and His DNA through being a new creature, you'll see yourself differently. Then you'll have more encounters because you'll be more in line with what heaven says about you. You'll experience more portal action—more words of knowledge, prophetic utterances, healings, visions, dreams, and supernatural encounters—when you realize you are seated with Christ in heavenly places (Eph. 2:6).

Saturate your mind with the truth that you have this position because of everything He's done for you, and you will begin to see yourself as holy, righteous, and pure. Making decisions in your life will become a fruit of simply having the identity of Christ. When all you want is to follow God and do what He says, you are living in the heavenly seat of ascension and the eternal realm of prosperity. Begin to see yourself like that and you will open yourself to more encounters.

People ask me all the time, "How do you have these encounters with heaven? I don't have any encounters. Nothing like this happens to me."

My response is to ask them, "Do you allow God to love you where you are? Do you allow yourself to receive the love and goodness of God? Do you allow Him to hug you? Do you allow Him to tell you how important you are to Him? Do you open your ears to what Jesus says about you because of what He did for you? Or do you close yourself off and tell yourself, 'I can't be that way because I don't do this or that right'? Is your world focused on statements such as 'Somebody talked bad about me, so that must be true'? In other words, do you live in a world of fear and doubt? Do you have negative self-talk?"

We're all living in a world of fear and doubt, but we must fight this with the truth of the Word to experience heavenly encounters. I'm not saying that heaven can't invade your space of negativity because it most certainly can in an instant. When Joseph was in a semiconscious dream state, heaven broke through his turmoil. Heaven will also break through to you when you begin to live a life in the eternal realm of prosperity. I will teach you more about this in later chapters so you can walk on a firm foundation of prosperity.

HIS FAVOR OPENS PORTALS

Mary also had an angelic encounter with heaven, but hers was different. She was not in a dream state. She had a heart of belief and gained the favor of God.

> In the sixth month of Elizabeth's pregnancy, God sent the angel Gabriel to Nazareth, a town in Galilee, to a virgin pledged to be married to a man named Joseph, a descendant of David. The virgin's name was Mary. The angel went to her and said, "Greetings, you who are highly favored! The Lord is with you."
>
> —Luke 1:26–28, niv

When the angel said, "you who are highly favored," the Word doesn't say Mary was shocked. It says,

> Mary was troubled at his words and wondered what kind of greeting this might be. But the angel said to her, "Do

not be afraid, Mary; you have found favor with God. You will conceive and give birth to a son, and you are to call him Jesus. He will be great and will be called the Son of the Most High. The Lord God will give him the throne of his father David, and he will reign over Jacob's descendants forever; his kingdom will never end."

"How will this be," Mary asked the angel, "since I am a virgin?"

—LUKE 1:29–34, NIV

In this passage, she's having a whole conversation with the angel. Then the Bible says,

The angel answered, "The Holy Spirit will come on you, and the power of the Most High will overshadow you. So the holy one to be born will be called the Son of God. Even Elizabeth your relative is going to have a child in her old age, and she who was said to be unable to conceive is in her sixth month. For no word from God will ever fail."

"I am the Lord's servant," Mary answered. "May your word to me be fulfilled." Then the angel left her.

—LUKE 1:35–38, NIV

That is one of my favorite parts in this whole passage as it says, "for no word from God will ever fail." And when Mary heard it, she submitted to it. Wow, talk about soul prosperity. Mary's soul was magnified, and she believed every word from God.

The heavenly portal opened because Mary had a heart of belief. The angel could visit her in that particular place, even in her conscious state. The angel showed up right in front of her and spoke to her one-on-one, and she received it. Yes, she may have been a little shaken, but the Word says she was more shaken about the greeting than she was about seeing the angel.

The Lord said Mary was highly favored, which means she had a highly favorable relationship with the Father. Mary must have said no to the things that tempted her or created issues in her life. God said she had favor. Wouldn't it be wonderful to have God say that about you?

Guess what? He does say that about you and me. I believe He's saying, "My bride, you're highly favored, you are My church. I love you so much. You are part of Me. I sent My Son, Jesus, so you would be ascended with Me to heavenly places in the spirit realm already." (See Ephesians 2:6.) If we soaked in that truth all the time, we would have more visitations from the supernatural. We would be supernatural instead of earthly in our responses.

MOUNT OF TRANSFIGURATION

God wants us to lead a life of being connected to heaven. I could share about many different portals, but let me focus on one more.

> After six days Jesus took with him Peter, James and John the brother of James, and led them up a high mountain by themselves. There he was transfigured before them. His face shone like the sun, and his clothes became as white as the light. Just then there appeared before them Moses and Elijah, talking with Jesus.
>
> —MATTHEW 17:1–3, NIV

That was a heavenly portal on a mountain. That Mount of Transfiguration is called Mount Tabor today. There are a lot of mountains in Israel, but this one is special. It was an open portal for heaven to the point that not only did Jesus shine bright, but Moses and Elijah were with them. Peter, James, and John, the brother of James, witnessed the portal being opened on the mountain, and they saw their Lord and Savior shining bright. They also saw Moses and Elijah, who lived in the heavenly realm yet descended to the earth. Heavenly portals are open to us daily in spaces, places, and by our heart belief in a moment.

Heavenly visitations will come when we're in our homes or other places worshipping. It happened to me. I got caught up to heaven in a portal a couple of times. Again, my story can be read in my book *Releasing Heaven*.

Since you learned from this chapter that you can open your heart as a portal to receive heavenly visitations, what should you be doing in your own life to encourage these encounters? There are spiritual disciplines such as praying, praising, worshipping, reading, and studying the Word of God. These disciplines provide habitations and environments that build our faith and expand our souls, making us prosperous of soul. The Word says, "Before I formed you in the womb I knew you, before you were born I set you apart; I appointed you as a prophet to the nations" (Jer. 1:5, NIV).

The Lord's plan for you includes that you be set apart, and He wants you to fulfill the assignment on your life. He wants you to believe in a great plan that He has for your life, so much that He sent Jesus to be the one to connect you to heaven every day and the realm of the eternal with Him, seated in the ascension seat and realm of prosperity. These places of soul prosperity will open the glory to be released, and signs, miracles, and wonders will be activated in the earthly realm. As we move forward I will continue to set a foundation where you can see how God made a way through Jesus to enter the heavenly realm and spark eternity to come to pass on earth.

PRAYERS FOR LOSS AND GRIEF

I encourage you to pray for heavenly portals to open for you. God wants you to walk in a prosperous soul that invites environments where the eternal can rule and reign and glory is released in the earth. You might be suffering for different reasons. Perhaps you are grieving the loss of family members, friends, businesses, and so on. You may be grieving over things that you can't control.

We are always concerned about people who are not saved. These concerns can be overwhelming, and we need to remember our ascension seat when we are in prayer. Let us pray from that seat.

> *Lord, heal our hearts today for the pain and brokenness we feel over the loss of our loved ones, friends, businesses, and others. We want to know that we are seated with You in the heavenly realm of eternal life. We speak eternal life over every area of earthly death that our loved ones and we ourselves are experiencing right now. Jesus, You made a way for eternal life, and we need life right now in the earthly realm. Open our eyes to see angels of comfort being released on our behalf. We thank You for Your Holy Spirit and love during this time of grief. We open our hearts to receive Your love. Thank You, Lord, that we are healed in Jesus' name and being raised to our heavenly seat with You as evidence of this.*

PRAYERS FOR OPEN PORTALS

> *Lord, we thank You for our ascension seat and the heavenly realm of prosperity You have positioned us to be in. We thank You, Father, because according to*

Your Word in Ephesians 2:6, we are seated with You in heavenly places, the doors are open already, and we have total access. Father, we praise and thank You in the mighty name of Jesus. We are grateful for open portals where heavenly visitations can come. We ask for encounters with angels. We ask for the faith to believe in Your goodness and love and what Jesus Christ has done for us that we might be saved, healed, and carriers of the good news, and so can those we love.

Just as the angels came to Mary and Elizabeth to say, "I have good news," let us be carriers of the good news. The joy of the Lord is our strength. Help us live in the joy of the Lord every single day because heaven is a joyous place, and we are in the prosperity realm. Living in joy means we are opening ourselves to portals of prosperity. Living in portals of prosperity means the glory of the Lord is being released. Anything less than that means we're not living out the inheritance that You have given us.

Father, we thank You in the mighty name of Jesus for all that You have done for us. Teach us, Lord, to pray from this place of ascension. All we ask is already ours because we are heavenly citizens and because You go to the Father on our behalf. We give You glory, honor, and praise for the dominion of life we are kingdom rulers of, and we are grateful that we can exercise our authority in the realm of the earth because You defeated sin, death, and the grave and ascended to the heavenly realm. All honor is Yours!

QUESTIONS *for* REFLECTION

1. Can you remember a dream or a particular place or season when you felt the overwhelming presence of God and entered a heavenly portal?

2. What attitude shift do you need personally so you can begin to see portals of heaven open for you?

3. What secret things is God speaking to your heart about the teaching you received in these chapters? Are you excited, apprehensive? Write any questions you have so you can look for God to reveal the answers as you continue forth.

CHAPTER 6

Realm of the Kingdom

IN THIS CHAPTER I want to share about the powerful realm of the kingdom and how you can operate in the eternal realm on earth. We have an earthly realm, and we have an eternal heavenly realm, and the eternal heavenly realm supersedes all that is on earth. The heavenly realm should be our first realm even though we are living in the earthly realm. We often want to escape the trials, circumstances, situations, and overwhelming things that happen to us in the earthly realm. But the Lord has made a way for us to be victorious over our circumstances, trials, and frustrations.

We can even be victorious over our weakness because God's power works in our weakness. This is a mystery in and of itself. When our flesh is weak, God is strong in us. Perhaps like many others, you can testify that at your weakest time you felt the strongest, but you can't explain it. It's because this is the development of intimacy with God that overflows in such a way that we are made strong. The apostle Paul tells us,

> Therefore I take pleasure in infirmities, in reproaches, in necessities, in persecutions, in distresses for Christ's sake: for when I am weak, then am I strong.
> —2 Corinthians 12:10

This truth will strengthen us and give us peace that surpasses all understanding. These types of supernatural connections with God are the outcomes of walking in the kingdom of heaven on earth. I want to talk to you about the realm of the kingdom of heaven and how we can walk in this realm of peace no matter our pain or weakness. This is a gift that the Lord gave us through His Son. This gift enables us to tread out the kingdom of heaven on earth. We do not have to wait for it. We can experience this phenomenon in the here and now. When Jesus died, resurrected, and ascended, He shifted things.

FAITH OPENS PORTALS TO THE KINGDOM

The church's job is to understand the kingdom of heaven and learn to walk in that place with Him daily, not having hindrances or boundaries, because Jesus removed them. When He died and resurrected, He overcame sin, death, and the grave. When He ascended, He positioned us for peace and rest. He positioned us to walk in the eternal realm of heaven while we're on earth. None of this is acquired except by faith. Faith comes by hearing the word of God (Rom. 10:17). The entire Word of God talks to us about how important faith is. Hebrews 11:1 says, "Now faith is the substance of things hoped for, the evidence of things not seen."

The Greek word for *substance* is *hupostasis*, which means

concrete essence or abstract security. In summary, it means tangible reality.[1] When we talk about faith, it's not an arbitrary thing. It's a tangible reality. It means when we're walking in the faith of God, we can see it, touch it, smell it, taste it, and hear it. We can have a relationship with God through faith, as it is a tangible reality. If your faith is still arbitrary or superficial, you need to ask God to open your mind to grab hold of how to activate a faith you can see and touch.

We have an initial faith in Jesus Christ as the One who has forgiven our sins. This initial faith opens a heavenly portal for walking in His power and living the Christian life. Faith is a key to access heaven, and the Bible talks about it from Genesis to Revelation. Jesus emphasized this with His disciples when He walked the earth. We must have faith. We must open our eyes to see that Jesus is in the Father, we are in Him, and Jesus is in us (John 14:20).

Remember, Jesus' disciples were Jews who had come to believe in Him as the Messiah. So when we read the Word of God, we must understand that He was talking to people who had learned that the Torah—the Pentateuch, the first five books of the Old Testament—was the way to the Father. That's why Jesus says,

> Think not that I am come to destroy the law, or the prophets: I am not come to destroy, but to fulfil. For verily I say unto you, Till heaven and earth pass, one jot or one tittle shall in no wise pass from the law, till all be fulfilled. Whosoever therefore shall break one of these least commandments, and shall teach men so, he shall be called the least in the kingdom of heaven: but whosoever shall do and teach them, the same shall be called great in the kingdom of heaven. For I say unto you, That except your righteousness shall

> exceed the righteousness of the scribes and Pharisees, ye
> shall in no case enter into the kingdom of heaven.
>
> —Matthew 5:17–20

Jesus is saying, "My Jewish brothers and sisters, you no longer have to look at the Torah as the only way to the Father. I am the way, the truth, and the life." Now that may not be as hard for Gentile Christians, who only know Jesus as Messiah and never grew up being taught that Moses and the Torah were the way to a relationship with the Father.

The Jews' relationship with God is through the law only. As Christians we understand our relationship with God differently. Jesus met the whole law of God. When we accept Jesus as our Lord and Savior, who has forgiven us of our sins and reconciled us to the Father through His shed blood, we have eternal access to heaven. We are Christ's body, and we are called to live by faith. As we do we enter a tangible reality. The Word says that faith is this tangible reality of things hoped for and evidence of things not seen (Heb. 11:1).

FULLNESS IS HEAVEN

Even though you have never been to heaven, you can experience the benefits of heaven in the here and now. You just need to understand that this is acquired by faith. This type of heavenly portal is a treasure you must hunt for. It is not something that comes easily. Why? Because we were born into sin, and as a result our souls are more attuned to the earthly realm than to the heavenly realm. Therefore faith is abstract. Jesus knew this, which is why He taught and trained for three years of earthly ministry. He wanted people to see things from God's perspective and make it their own.

The Lord desires that we as Christ's body learn to walk in the fullness of heaven. We can walk in fullness when we know and understand the kingdom. Let's read what Jesus said about it.

> Again, the kingdom of heaven is like unto treasure hid in a field; the which when a man hath found, he hideth, and for joy thereof goeth and selleth all that he hath, and buyeth that field.
>
> —MATTHEW 13:44

Jesus said He is the gate for the sheep, and His work was to share the kingdom of heaven with us so we could understand and access the gate that enables us to walk as citizens of heaven on earth. When Jesus was speaking about this to His disciples and other people, He hadn't yet died. Still, He was telling them, "This is what heaven is." Jesus was saying to them, "When I die, resurrect, and ascend, it will position you to have access to a heavenly gateway by faith."

He says that the kingdom of heaven is like a treasure hidden in a field, and when a man finds it he buys the whole field. Jesus is explaining the epitome of fullness. This guy wasn't satisfied just with the treasure. He wanted the whole field. Jesus is telling us, "It's not even about the treasure you're hunting; it's about all that comes with the treasure—the total, complete fullness that comes with the treasure."

We're so focused on what we can get our hands on in a moment because we live in a place of lack. Jesus is trying to tell the disciples and the rest of the people that the kingdom of heaven is more significant than just a treasure. It's an expanse like a field. This man who found the treasure went and hid it again, then he bought the field. He realized it. He realized that it is not just a treasure; it's the fullness that comes with the treasure. That's the real treasure. It emcompasses everything, with nothing missing and nothing broken. This is the meaning of the Hebrew word *shalom*, which you may remember means complete, total in its entirety. That's the kingdom of heaven: nothing missing, nothing broken.

God is offering that kingdom of heaven to you today. When your body dies, your spirit and soul go to heaven, and there is fullness in that place, but you can experience that fullness now in your soul.

Jesus also shared a parable that says,

> Again, the kingdom of heaven is like unto a merchant man, seeking goodly pearls: Who, when he had found one pearl of great price, went and sold all that he had, and bought it.
>
> —MATTHEW 13:45–46

Both men—the merchant and the one looking for the treasure—were looking for something because they were not satisfied with the way things were and believed there was something better. They had faith that there was something better. This merchant looked for fine pearls. When he found one of great value, he sold everything he had to buy it. Why? Because to him fullness, completion, and totality were in that one purchase. If you want to grab hold of tangible faith—the substance of things hoped for and evidence of things not seen—then you need to understand this parable.

Unless God has given you a vision, encounter, or dream of a hope and a future, something better in the field of your life, you have not had the opportunity to see heaven. You must grab hold of your field simply by believing in what Jesus says and

His nature of goodness and love. If Jesus speaks of this message from heaven, it must be good.

MY TESTIMONY OF MINISTRY CALLING

I remember many years ago when the Lord called me to ministry. He began to send me on treasure hunts. I've been on lots of treasure hunts with the Lord. I'm still on treasure hunts with Him daily. He gives me certain things, and I must research until I have all the information. In one instance I remember dealing with some challenging things in my life because He was calling me into ministry, and there was a purification process I had to go through.

I call the years when my kids were tiny my "desert years"— not because my kids didn't give me joy, but because I wondered whether I had another purpose in life aside from that. I had always been an academic who had gone to school and studied hard in many different areas. In that season I found myself at home with my three small children under three and a half, which was a total blessing. But there was a hunger in me for more.

I can remember thinking, "Watching animated movies, playing with dolls, throwing balls, and having tea parties with my kids is so awesome. But Lord, I need to know there is more for me than what I'm doing at this point." He was guiding me into that place of saying there is more, but I also needed to commit to the journey that would take me to the land of more. The Lord was building in me a godly striving, a continued desire to seek Him.

> It is the glory of God to conceal a matter, but the glory of kings is to search out a matter.
>
> —Proverbs 25:2, nkjv

The more I sought Him and the treasure of His Word, the more I found Him in the Word. I think people seek just a little bit and find just a little bit, but then the enemy trips them up and they decide they will not search anymore.

God used the times when the enemy was tripping me up or bringing my sin right in front of my face to purify me. The Lord was having me deal with my issues, and He would say to me, "Don't quit. Just keep looking!" The enemy wanted to side-track me and get me focused on myself so I wouldn't search for treasure or try to find the truth God had said in His Word. But God was driving me to a place of knowing more, and He was building a tenacity for the journey. You've got to commit to the journey. You must continue to mine for gold and look for the treasure, no matter how difficult your situation gets.

You must come to a place where you realize it's not your difficult situation; it's whether you will mine in the middle of it, whether you will look for the gold treasure even though you're in a difficult spot. No matter how difficult my life got, I just kept mining and saying, "There's got to be some truth here. There's some truth about me. There's some truth about You, Lord. There's some truth about my family. There's some truth about my purpose and destiny. There is some truth here, and I will not quit looking for it until I have the answers, until I encounter You in the middle of it."

Guess what? He was faithful, and He's still faithful today. Don't think for one minute that I'm not still asking Him just as I did all those years ago, "Lord, show me more, teach me more, reveal more. There are more things we've got to work on. There's more we must do here." I am always on the hunt.

Jesus shared in these parables that these guys were searching for the kingdom of heaven because they knew they would encounter something full and complete. This hunt was for the kingdom of heaven on earth.

KINGDOM RULERSHIP

What is the kingdom of heaven? The Greek word for *kingdom* is *basileia,* and it means the reign or royalty of heaven.[2] *Basileia* is broken down to the word *basileus,* which means the sovereign power or foundation of the Lord.[3] This means the kingdom of heaven is a royal reign of His sovereign power; it's a foundation. Then you can break the word down just a little bit more to the word *basis,* which means pace or foot, as in keeping pace while walking.[4] When Jesus is saying the kingdom of heaven is like a treasure in a field, He's saying that the kingdom is like a royal reign of sovereign power, a foundation we acquire when we keep pace and our feet keep walking. This is a kingdom where we find the treasure of fullness, completeness, and shalom peace.

I have assessed this for quite some time. When we talk about ascension, we mean that the kingdom of heaven is an extension of the ascension. If we want to experience the kingdom of heaven today, we must be lifted from the earthly realm into the heavenly realm by a heavenly portal or access point by faith in our mind. No matter what you're going through—no matter what situation you find yourself in or what your sphere of influence looks like—you can see and respond to heaven while you're doing things in the earthly realm.

There is an open heaven all the time with no boundary whatsoever. Kingdom living means there isn't a boundary between the earth and heaven because Jesus broke that boundary. He broke that veil. I believe God's giving you a revelation now, and you can take this revelation and continue to advance on it. Your ability to advance this revelation depends on how much you're willing to mine for treasure. It's an individual thing. When you go to church and hear a great word, if you do nothing with what you've heard, you've wasted your time. If you don't work that word, you won't see that word work for you.

When Jesus walked the earth He was the kingdom of heaven walking into the earthly realm, which did not know heaven. He was the example. The here and now is true for us today. You can walk in the earthly realm, and you can have heaven with you every step of the way as though there's no barrier whatsoever. You can be working in your kitchen, and your kitchen can be a realm of heaven. As you're preparing food, as you're fellowshipping with family and friends, it's a realm of heaven right there in the middle of the earth. You might look around and say, well, this is about as earthly as it can be, but that's from a natural viewpoint. That's not from a spiritual viewpoint. Because you are a portal or gateway for the kingdom of heaven, you're there, so heaven is there. When you're doing something or connecting with people, whatever you're doing, it can be the kingdom of heaven made manifest while you're here in the earthly realm.

Ask the Lord to show you the fullness of your environment, with Him being the maximum weight of that moment. Each moment you spend on earth—whatever it is you're doing right now—you're defying the power of the earthly realm. You're in a heavenly space where everything expands. It's total fullness—everything's complete, final, and total, and nothing is missing or broken.

FULLNESS IN ETERNAL TIME

Every day of human life something is missing or broken because of the fall of man. Adam and Eve lived in the Garden of Eden without fear of death. This reality meant that time was like heaven in that they existed in a world without end. Time was an element of forever, and it was whole and not slipping away quickly as it is to us now. Once they ate the forbidden fruit a realm of death entered, time was cut short, and redemption was needed.

This meant God needed to create a way to meet us in earthly time so that He could save us and bring us back to relationship with Him, and we would then again enter the portal of eternal time. Eternal time is heavenly time; it is whole and complete forever, with nothing missing or broken. Therefore, if we are now in the eternal time portal, there's no more fear of death or a race for time.

Do you ever feel as if there is not enough time and you are always running out of time, like a time warp? We constantly fight with time and lose. We just lost one second, two seconds, three seconds, and so on. This is an element of the fall of man. You will never get that time back. Right? The earthly realm is constantly stealing.

You might be thinking, "I live this every day. I am so time conscious." When Jesus performed all these miracles on earth, He was not thinking in earthly fear of time; He thought eternally every moment. He agreed to come into the earth's time, but He saw it from a different perspective. He saw it from eternal time. It was time without end. Jesus factored in His death happening in the earthly realm but spoke of it as breaking a barrier where now eternal time would become the norm. Jesus told His disciples,

> Anyone who loves me will obey my teaching. My Father will love them, and we will come to them and make our home with them. Anyone who does not love me will not obey my teaching. These words you hear are not my own; they belong to the Father who sent me. All this I have spoken while still with you. But the Advocate, the Holy

Spirit, whom the Father will send in my name, will teach you all things and will remind you of everything I have said to you. Peace I leave with you; my peace I give you. I do not give to you as the world gives. Do not let your hearts be troubled and do not be afraid. You heard me say, "I am going away and I am coming back to you." If you loved me, you would be glad that I am going to the Father, for the Father is greater than I. I have told you now before it happens, so that when it does happen you will believe.

—John 14:23–29, niv

Jesus speaks of making His home with us in the earthly time zone while He has entered the eternal time zone. He speaks of "going away and coming back" and tells us about eternal things before they happen in the earth realm. He is teaching that fear is a result of death, and death robs us of eternal life, but He has come to give us His peace where we know that time is forever and will never end because of what He has done. Now we can partake of the benefits of eternal or endless time in these bodies because of the Holy Spirit He has sent to us. He is trying to help the disciples see that He is defying death, which means He is redeeming time. Ephesians 5:15–17 reads:

See then that ye walk circumspectly, not as fools, but as wise, redeeming the time, because the days are evil. Wherefore be ye not unwise, but understanding what the will of the Lord is.

We are called to walk circumspectly as a result of this knowledge of the kingdom of heaven. Death stops time, which is why we fear. If we see time as only earthly then we rush through life. This is in our DNA; it is part of our soul from the fall of man.

were only relevant to Jesus, then why teach us to walk in miracles, healings, and representations of the kingdom of heaven? Jesus knew that for the kingdom of heaven to impact earth through us, His disciples, these truths had to be a reality in the moment and more so because He died, resurrected, and ascended. That's where we are today.

The Lord said to the apostle John,

> After this I looked, and, behold, a door was opened in heaven: and the first voice which I heard was as it were of a trumpet talking with me; which said, Come up hither, and I will shew thee things which must be hereafter.
>
> —REVELATION 4:1

We must change our thinking from earthly to heavenly. If [yo]u don't understand what that means, ask the Lord because [the]re's a whole lot of treasure He wants to pour out to you. Don't [be] lazy about these truths. Go for your treasure and spend a [coup]le of hours finding out what this kingdom of heaven is and [how] it impacts your life. Ask Him, "How does this impact my [? H]ow does this impact my relationship?" I asked Him those [questio]ns, and it opened a heavenly portal for me to walk in on [eart]h. It changed how I walked.

[He is] pleased to give you the kingdom, and that isn't just [when yo]u said yes to Jesus when you got saved. You didn't say [yes one] time and that was it. No, there is so much more to [it. R]edemption is not one time; it is every day. It is in the [now] because we're living eternally. This moment right [now is eterna]l. It's a moment that's occurring right now from a [heavenly persp]ective and an earthly perspective. We're on earth, [and] in the heavenly realm right now, fully redeemed.

Jesus defied this realm of death and redeemed time, and now He expects all of His disciples to live the same way once they have the Holy Spirit.

Jesus' eyes could see a heavenly perspective where everything is already whole and complete. Because of what Jesus did in His death, resurrection, and ascension, we are right now in a heavenly space redeemed also because we are His body. We're seated with Him in heavenly places as Ephesians 2:6 says.

Look at your own life through the truth of what Jesus has said. Is it not true that because of His death, resurrection, and ascension this very moment of your life is eternal, and you don't have to race through it? Is it not true that the enemy wants to rob you of this eternal moment by making it a lack moment of earthly time and bringing in fear?

At this moment you can expand in the fullness of eternal time. You can rest in the fullness of eternal time by choosing to believe and live in that heavenly eternal time space now. You can buy the whole field instead of just the treasure. Why? Because in this space of the kingdom of heaven is the fullness of everything you need; nothing is missing and nothing is broken, so you don't have to fix it.

If you don't have to fix something, such as time, because it is redeemed, then it's total and complete right now. You are now living in a time zone where, if you choose to move forward, you will be a blessing of redemption depositing in the earth realm. You will not try to retrieve the moment out of fear of losing it, which is ultimately death. If you're in the heavenly realm while you're walking on earth, you are in the pace and gait and movement of heaven though you are on earth. And that's what the kingdom of heaven is all about: the rule, the royalty, and the reign from the foundation where everything can be full and complete, even if in the natural realm it looks broken.

I CAN'T GET NO SATISFACTION

From the last paragraph, you have grasped that eternal time is your new way of living. This concept exists by faith. We know there is a new way of living now, and Jesus redeemed time and made things complete when He died, resurrected, and ascended. Now we can apply this to how we perceive issues in our life. As I shared with you in earlier chapters, we are always analyzing what is broken or needs to be fixed. It is how our minds work as a result of the fall of man. It is simply humanity. Every thought in our minds is from lack, which robs us of peace and keeps us in a constant state of toiling. This is why every thought needs redemption.

Take some time and just analyze your thoughts. They are probably about what you don't have or where you're going next. There's no satisfaction in that. But the space of the kingdom of heaven is fullness, and it's all complete; it's total. Your viewpoint changes.

How can you live now that time is redeemed? In a world full of evil and sickness and things needing to be fixed, we must be empowered by understanding that Jesus knew the kingdom of heaven was at hand (Matt. 4:17).

Jesus knew that for the three years He came into His ministry. He kept telling the disciples, "Listen, watch Me, and do what I do. See the things that I do. You will do greater things than these." You've got to grasp the revelation of the fullness if you're ever going to step into the kingdom of heaven on earth. It's not possible any other way. If something is missing or broken, it's not heaven. In heaven, nothing is missing or broken; it is redeemed. So begin to think eternally that Jesus mended everything broken.

We must see things complete in order to live as this truth will help fix the earth. Then we will heaven encounters and see signs, miracles, and

This is what living by real, tangible faith—t faith—is all about. What I'm talking about is ta when we seek the treasure and agree with God moment is heavenly. Then the glory of the Lord because, in the realm of the kingdom on ear missing or broken.

I know your head is spinning in a thousand tions to grasp this. You are probably thinking, " understand. I've got this problem and that prob That is everyday earth living from a viewpoint tion. But start approaching it from a heavenly st ness, completeness, nothing missing, nothing br is redeemed and hidden with Christ in God. T meet you at that moment. If heaven meets y then how will you respond? Will you b it? No, there's no freaking out in heave wholeness. No one's even crying becau broken. But that's what He's offerin or present earth realm, which is w that I explained earlier.

This is a concept we must in the earthly realm because open to us.

You and I can experi now. It is ours because time and expects us it were not true, Je walking the earth

We must see things complete in order to live as He lived. Then this truth will help fix the earth. Then we will walk in open-heaven encounters and see signs, miracles, and wonders.

This is what living by real, tangible faith—the substance of faith—is all about. What I'm talking about is tangibly acquired when we seek the treasure and agree with God that even this moment is heavenly. Then the glory of the Lord can be released because, in the realm of the kingdom on earth, nothing is missing or broken.

I know your head is spinning in a thousand different directions to grasp this. You are probably thinking, "Wait, you don't understand. I've got this problem and that problem." I get it. That is everyday earth living from a viewpoint of no redemption. But start approaching it from a heavenly standpoint: fullness, completeness, nothing missing, nothing broken. Your life is redeemed and hidden with Christ in God. Then heaven will meet you at that moment. If heaven meets you at that moment, then how will you respond? Will you be freaked out about it? No, there's no freaking out in heaven. There is peace and wholeness. No one's even crying because nothing is missing or broken. But that's what He's offering us in the here and now or present earth realm, which is what He said in John 14:23–29 that I explained earlier.

This is a concept we must grasp if we are to live in peace in the earthly realm because this is how the portals of heaven open to us.

You and I can experience victorious living in the here and now. It is ours because He paid the price for us; He redeemed time and expects us to walk diligently in that (Eph. 5:15–16). If it were not true, Jesus would not have said so. Instead He was walking the earth saying, "This is the kingdom of heaven." If it

were only relevant to Jesus, then why teach us to walk in miracles, healings, and representations of the kingdom of heaven? Jesus knew that for the kingdom of heaven to impact earth through us, His disciples, these truths had to be a reality in the moment and more so because He died, resurrected, and ascended. That's where we are today.

The Lord said to the apostle John,

> After this I looked, and, behold, a door was opened in heaven: and the first voice which I heard was as it were of a trumpet talking with me; which said, Come up hither, and I will shew thee things which must be hereafter.
>
> —REVELATION 4:1

We must change our thinking from earthly to heavenly. If you don't understand what that means, ask the Lord because there's a whole lot of treasure He wants to pour out to you. Don't be lazy about these truths. Go for your treasure and spend a couple of hours finding out what this kingdom of heaven is and how it impacts your life. Ask Him, "How does this impact my job? How does this impact my relationship?" I asked Him those questions, and it opened a heavenly portal for me to walk in on the earth. It changed how I walked.

He is pleased to give you the kingdom, and that isn't just because you said yes to Jesus when you got saved. You didn't say yes for one time and that was it. No, there is so much more to the story. Redemption is not one time; it is every day. It is in the here and now because we're living eternally. This moment right now is eternal. It's a moment that's occurring right now from a heavenly perspective and an earthly perspective. We're on earth, but we're seated in the heavenly realm right now, fully redeemed.

THE GLORY RELEASED

How will you be a ruler in the kingdom of heaven if you don't even know how the kingdom of heaven works? It's not just being nice to your neighbor, which is a beautiful thing, but there's way more than that. We are called to go forth and minister the gospel with our voice and administer the gospel with our hands and feet, right? Sure, you can do good works, but God doesn't want you to do good works that deplete you. He wants you to do good works from a place of fullness and abundance, a place overflowing with heaven. It's through the heavenly portal—which opens the eternal heavenly realm into the earth—that we can begin to walk in the fullness, and then He will do the work through you. We will be united with Him as one flesh doing it together—He and His body, the church.

The fullness is the glory pouring through us into the earthly realm. Psalm 37:5 says, "Commit thy way unto the Lord; trust also in him; and he shall bring it to pass." The work that He does comes in the glory. His work comes when we recognize that the heavenly realm and the earth are not separated; they become one in Jesus. The only difference is how we think about it. It is truth in our minds.

You are the connection between heaven and earth. And if you think more heaven than you think earth, you will see the miracles and healings that you're asking God to see. You will be able to take a stand for your family. You will be able to walk victoriously, but you need to have fullness, an understanding of how Jesus redeemed time.

The church of Jesus Christ, who has ascended with Him and is seated with Him in heavenly places, must get a new frame of reference. The Lord is speaking this to us because He is accelerating things. Have you noticed how the years seem to go faster than ever before? That's a spiritual thing. God is accelerating things, and we must learn to manage our earthly time from an eternal time perspective.

So buy the field and not just the treasure. Buy the pearl of great price, which is the truths surrounding the kingdom of heaven. Live out the fullness of redemption of time.

We can talk all we want about seeing great things happen on earth. The Lord is calling the church to change its perspective of heaven and begin operating in the here and now. I know this is a difficult teaching that can challenge one's faith. I want to pray for you to be open in your mind to what you read so you can step into the heavenly realm in the here and now.

PRAYER FOR A HEAVENLY PERSPECTIVE

You are awesome, Lord. We thank You, Jesus, that You have made a way for us to be in total union with You through Your redemptive sacrifice. We are seated with You in heavenly places, and those heavenly places are in the earthly realm as well. When we activate the heavenly portal of faith, there is no divide, Lord Jesus, as we are one in You when we position ourselves as seated with You in these heavenly places, manifesting in the environments that You've given us in the earthly realm. I ask You to open the spiritual eyes of each of us so our spiritual sight, hearing, smell, taste, and touch will be revealed in dreams and visions and give us an understanding of the eternal heavenly realm. This revelation in our souls will help us walk in fullness and completeness, where nothing is missing and nothing is broken. We bind any spirits of doubt or lack of understanding on us right now in the mighty name of Jesus. Father, release in us the faith and understanding to receive the tangibility of the kingdom of heaven.

I ask You to retrain our minds to a heavenly understanding and the realm of eternal time. Keep us moving with You at that accelerated pace that You've called us to, where the kingdom of heaven moves, expands, and grows on earth. We praise You. We thank You for what Your Son, Jesus, did, because we don't even have a message to share about the kingdom of heaven without Him. There's only one way to heaven: through the shed blood of Jesus Christ. Father, teach us to take steps to live in the supernatural realm of heaven on earth in Jesus' name. Amen.

QUESTIONS *for* REFLECTION

1. What is missing and broken in your life today? Do you believe these broken places can be made whole in your mind as you understand the redemptive power of Jesus' death, resurrection, and ascension? Explain here.

2. What mind shifts do you need to build your faith to walk in fullness and completion?

3. What treasure hunts does the Lord have you on? List them below. If you are not on a treasure hunt, ask the Lord to put you on one. Then you will know Him more.

CHAPTER 7

Walking as Citizens of Heaven, Part 1

E HAVE A difficult time understanding the realm of eternal living on earth. It is more heavenly than earthly, and we are so programmed to walk earthly. That is our humanity. Jesus was human, but He walked heavenly. He wants His disciples to walk heavenly, think eternally, and exercise kingdom citizenship with kingdom power on earth, just as He did as our example.

This chapter is the cornerstone of this book. Walking in the heavenly realm opens portals that reveal eternity in our past and provide a foundation for eternity in our present and future. I am so excited because these are truths from heaven for those who want to walk in kingdom citizenship on earth. The incredible encounters I have had with the Lord to scribe this teaching have forever changed my life. My soul is functioning at another level of prosperity as a result. I've seen more of God's glory released and experienced more awe and wonder at His love and goodness for His people. These revelations enable me to explain the keys to the heavenly portals.

FAITH ACTIVATION PRAYER

I want to start this chapter off with prayer. Some things can be taught, and some can be caught. I want you to catch this. Until you catch this and make it your own, you will never be able to walk in it. Catching it is a supernatural thing. Right where you are, please pray the following prayer.

> *Father, I praise You and thank You right now in the mighty name of Jesus. As Your word comes forth, it shall not return void but shall accomplish the purpose for which You sent it. Father, I ask right now for You to help me catch this word through sight, sound, smell, taste, and touch in the heavenly realm. Give me great revelation from heaven in the mighty name of Jesus. Open the eyes of my heart that I might be enlightened to see and hear this word in the spiritual realm so that my faith is increased.*

Now tell the Lord that you want to know how to operate in the eternal realm while you live in the earthly realm, and you want to walk as a kingdom citizen on earth. OK, now you are ready!

YOU ARE A CITIZEN OF HEAVEN FIRST

> But our citizenship is in heaven. And we eagerly await a Savior from there, the Lord Jesus Christ.
>
> —Philippians 3:20, niv

We are made citizens of heaven because of Jesus' death, resurrection, and ascension. His ascension makes you a citizen of heaven because at His resurrection He broke the power of sin, death, and the grave. When He ascended, He took us, His church, with Him. Now this is our new seat, our new residency, our new home.

When you call yourself a citizen of heaven, that means you believe—though your physical body is here in the earthly realm—you have given your heart and mind to Jesus. If your heart and mind are with Jesus, you are where He is, and because He is ascended, you are seated with Him. You are now with your groom, your heavenly husband, Jesus. You are with your Father and King from a heavenly perspective, even though your body is on earth. These truths made Jesus' ministry powerful.

When He came to do signs, miracles, and wonders, we saw His physical body on earth, and He integrated with us that way, but His heart and mind never left His home with His Father God. That's why He was so sad on the cross. He was separated from His Father because He bore the sins of the world. There are different translations for what He said on the cross. Some theologians say in Matthew 27:46 that He said in a loud voice, "Eli, Eli lema sabachthani," meaning, "My God, my God, why have you forsaken me?" However, the English translation of this Aramaic phrase is, "My God, My God, for this I was destined."[1]

But either way, when sin was put on Jesus, He had to be separated from His Father, which was extremely painful for Him. It is extremely painful for you when you know you're not walking with the Lord, isn't it? If you are a citizen of heaven, you are in a relationship with the Lord, where He is Father. You know when you have divided or separated that relationship with Him because you'll start feeling anxiety, fear, and frustration. You'll feel as if God does not hear you and your prayers have a lid on them. That's painful when He's our Father and our God and we only want to be with Him.

In the apostle Paul's letter to the church at Philippi, he was giving them a play-by-play of progressive revelation he was receiving. Paul wanted the Philippians to understand the power of walking as citizens of heaven in the earthly realm. It was a necessary part of the kingdom impact they were called to have on earth. This type of word would shake the church out of its lack mindset to a place of fullness and completion, which is where we need to be walking every day of our life as kingdom citizens.

We should be walking in the joy of the Lord. The joy of the Lord is a normal thing. It is not an occasional fleeting moment. It is your life because He is your life, and your life is hidden with Christ in God. The Lord wants you to know these things about His goodness. He's good all the time. He's not good just because we think He's good in one moment of our lives. He's good because it's part of His nature. Under this revelation we change. God interacts with us from an eternal perspective and beckons us to change our earthly thinking. When we search for these treasures we'll begin to grab hold of who He is. I believe that you can grab hold of who He is. When that happens, expanse happens and we are magnified in our souls. Then we begin to feel the fullness and the completion and walk in it by faith. It becomes a substance we can touch and feel, and thus the eternal realm affects the earthly realm.

HOW TO LIVE NOW

This is done first in our souls—our mind, will, and emotions. Then it is carried out in our walk on earth. The central part of your soul is your mind. Your mind exists in your brain, a physical organ. The mind is a cognitive way of thinking inside the physical aspect of your brain. The mind also houses your emotions and your will. So your will or volition is also inside the brain. To access heaven, from the perspective of doing what the apostle Paul says and being a citizen of heaven on earth, we must learn to train our minds. The things I will teach you in the rest of this book are possible, but your mind must be willing to be disciplined.

Some people have very undisciplined minds. Now, it's not our fault. We are born undisciplined; it's human nature. We're born with a volition that moves at the whim of whatever. A baby will move at whatever whim. They just go out in whatever direction, and they're quickly moving from one thing to another. As we grow older we should develop a framework in which we're very disciplined in our minds. This concept is called metacognition. It means you think about what you're thinking about. You can know and understand at those levels of thought.

Have you ever read a whole chapter in a book and then said, "I don't even know what I just read"? That is an undisciplined mind. This happens because your mind was unfocused as you read the pages, and you thought you were taking something into your mind, but you weren't there. You got through the whole project and thought, "What did I just read?" We do this a lot when we're driving. We call it autopilot when we automatically move, but we don't have to be thinking about where we are going or what we are doing.

It's kind of scary to be a citizen of heaven because you are called to operate in the earthly realm with a disciplined mind from the eternal realm perspective. You're already a citizen of heaven, but now you will activate portals that help you experience the benefits of that citizenship. You must have a trained mind to activate portals and realize the benefits of being a citizen of heaven.

This is the place where we see the earthly realm change because we are a part of it. We have a disciplined mind, which means we are single-minded. We live in the present; we're not thinking about the past or future, but the present. A disciplined mind doesn't have its thoughts on the last minute or on the minute to come. It has its thoughts on the moment.

If you're like most people, you spend your life dwelling on what just happened in the last five minutes and then thinking about what will happen in the next five minutes, and you are never in the moment. It's normal to do this. Remember from an earlier chapter I explained that when the enemy tricked Adam and Eve and humanity fell into sin, we entered a time warp. This time warp means that our minds are always on yesterday or tomorrow, but never on the moment. That's why Jesus is so powerful: He was able to live and breathe in the moment of earthly time while holding an eternal time perspective. He has now redeemed this time warp for us.

Those who wrote the Word of God, such as the apostle Paul, received their training and became master trainers, telling us how to walk this out. If we have a disciplined mind, we know that we need to live in the present moment. For example, imagine I'm standing in front of you and I start walking. I'm in the moment of walking. I'm not paying attention to where I just came from, and I'm not paying attention to where I'm going. I'm paying attention to walking at this moment now. This is experiencing the moment of heaven in this timeframe. As I walk at this moment, I am bringing the eternal realm of life into the earthly realm of lack, poverty, and death. I am walking in redemption of time.

I'm not in the past, and I'm not in the future. I'm in a specific moment—that has already been written—being carried out in present time. I will show you this from the Word of God. It's already been written, which means it's already complete. Therefore, I don't have to push forward or backward because it's already in that moment. Keep that in your mind. Even if you're in a state of confusion from this teaching, it's OK. Just keep that in your mind. Because the more we get into the Word, the more it will break this down for you. You'll realize why kingdom citizens need to know and understand these concepts of eternal time and what it does to our will.

ROYAL REIGN

In the last chapter I shared that in the Bible, everywhere you see kingdom or kingdom of heaven, the Greek word is *basileia*. It means royal reign.[2] It's also broken down to *basileus*, which means sovereign power or foundation, and further broken down to the root word *basis*, meaning pace or foot. This means that the kingdom of heaven exists at our pace. Therefore, you are walking in heaven on earth because the kingdom of heaven has arrived. The reign of the kingdom is already here. You've been given royal reign everywhere you go.

The enemy wants you to forget that you're a genuine citizen of heaven. He wants to remind you that you are part of the generations of Adam and Eve. This means you have what's called a sinful nature. But Jesus counteracts that sinful nature, including our undisciplined mind, which is focused on lack. Jesus' death, burial, and resurrection overrule the disobedience and sin in the Garden of Eden.

We come to this revelatory place where we're asked to walk as heavenly citizens, which means we must take on a whole new identity. We must understand there are always open heavenly portals, or gateways, surrounding us every minute of our earthly lives. There is no barrier between us and heaven at any given time because redemption has occurred. We never leave the eternal heavenly realm; we just don't believe this fully in our minds. We must be trained to this truth. We need heavenly portals activated by faith so we can bring eternity into the present. Jesus lived His life like this, and He wanted to show the disciples and us how powerful this truth was. This is why He did so many miracles on earth. He lived out of the heavenly realm into the earthly realm. Portals help us activate these truths so that heaven can be made manifest in the earth. Remember we access portals through believing the Word and understanding in our minds. Technically, because Jesus was our example and His death, resurrection, and ascension was sufficient, we have never left the eternal realm. Once we receive Jesus as Savior, we have the power of the Holy Spirit inside us, and we are sealed in the ascension life. We now must be trained to live this way. This is what kingdom citizens know!

That's why we have so many carnal Christians. As people get saved in their spirit man, they never allow their minds to be renewed and their souls to be transformed. That's why they still have the same behaviors they had the day they got saved. They never took time to allow the Word to change them into the likeness of Christ and live as kingdom citizens.[3]

This is a training process. It's training for reigning. It's training for the battle of the mind and for the citizens of heaven. We are called to do battle by exercising our identity as kingdom citizens with kingdom authority. Kingdom citizens don't get upset about the past or the future. We are citizens of an eternal heaven, and we know it is being made manifest on earth.

ATTITUDE OF HEAVEN

Take a breath. Now take another breath. It is easier than we think. That's what it's like to be in the kingdom. The kingdom is not self-confidence but God-confidence. It's knowing that what Jesus did was enough, and we don't have to be tripped up. Now, this mind between our ears is slacking. It lives in the realm of lack and poverty and always thinks that something is wrong and must be fixed. This is a sinful effect of the fall of man. It is a consequence of sin. We live in a mind of self-doubt and a nagging need to fix brokenness. This is one reason we need redemption. Our earthly mind is never satisfied with where it's at. It's always either looking ahead for ways to get more or looking back at when we had less. Don't fret. It's OK. That's sinful nature. However, that's not the realm of the kingdom.

The realm of the kingdom is complete, whole, and total, with nothing missing and nothing broken, which means you wouldn't be thinking about what's broken because nothing is missing and broken. You wouldn't think about what you need or don't have because you already have it; it is redeemed.

Everything is finished, and because it is, when we talk about the heavenly realm and eternity and walking as citizens of heaven, that's a state of mind we must choose to walk in all the time.

> Let us therefore, as many as be perfect, be thus minded: and if in any thing ye be otherwise minded, God shall reveal even this unto you.
>
> —Philippians 3:15

The apostle Paul is saying that we need to have a standard in which we're living in the attitude of a heavenly citizen. He is saying if you don't have this attitude, you need to get it. Our attitudes are locked in our soul (mind, will, and emotions).

> Nevertheless, whereto we have already attained, let us walk
> by the same rule, let us mind the same thing. Brethren, be
> followers together of me, and mark them which walk so as
> ye have us for an ensample.
> —PHILIPPIANS 3:16–17

He will give an example of what it means to walk as obedient. He's saying, "Listen, brothers, I want you to follow my example and be those who walk according to the pattern. Please pay attention to those who know how to walk, for many walk as enemies of the cross." In other words, many are not good examples.

> (For many walk, of whom I have told you often, and now
> tell you even weeping, that they are the enemies of the
> cross of Christ: Whose end is destruction, whose God is
> their belly, and whose glory is in their shame, who mind
> earthly things.)
> —PHILIPPIANS 3:18–19

The apostle Paul is sorrowful. Have you ever been with people whose glory is in their shame? When people are proud of shameful things, we are to weep. Paul is not talking about citizens of heaven. He's talking about those who mind earthly things.

> For our conversation is in heaven; from whence also we
> look for the Saviour, the Lord Jesus Christ: Who shall
> change our vile body, that it may be fashioned like unto
> his glorious body, according to the working whereby he is
> able even to subdue all things unto himself.
> —PHILIPPIANS 3:20–21

The fact of the matter is he's talking about two different people here. He's talking about citizens of heaven, which we are, and he's talking about those who have chosen not to be citizens of heaven. What does this mean? It means if you're a citizen of heaven, then you will not be glorying in your shame. You will not always be thinking about what you will eat and drink, or where these kinds of earthly needs are to be met all the time. You instead are trusting the Lord to provide.

Now, if you still fall into that category and you're saved, it just means you're a citizen of heaven who doesn't know your identity. You are acting carnal and worldly but not royal. That's OK because somebody needs to tell you that's not you. If you received Jesus as your Lord and Savior, let your mind be on heavenly things. Your focus is not on your belly or fleshly desires but on bringing the kingdom of heaven to earth.

MIND ON HEAVENLY THINGS

Throughout this whole passage the apostle Paul is saying we're not people concerned with the flesh. He's saying we are those with the attitude of the royalty of the kingdom of heaven. And he begins to put emphasis here on the mind. Now, the Greek word for *mind* is *phroneo*, and it means to exercise your mind. It means being mentally disposed, going in a specific direction, being interested in oneself, being concerned, or disobedience. It is broken down into the Greek word *phren*, which means the feelings or sensitive nature as in the midriff, our feelings, and the cognitive faculties.[4] Therefore, our minds can either care for heavenly things and the things of God, or our minds can care for fleshly things, which are not of God.

This does not mean that God does not care about fleshy things, such as meeting our daily needs on earth; on the contrary, it means He cares so much for us that He will make a way every day from an eternal heavenly realm. We need to stop ruminating on the things we need because that means our lack mindset from the fall of man is ruling us. We need to rule our minds and rule the kingdom of heaven on earth, and not be ruled by the mind in lack, or the undisciplined mind. We as kingdom citizens are not to have our affections set on the world, but this mind should be trained to have its affections set on the things of life and heaven. The apostle Paul says that we are heavenly creatures who need to have our minds focused on the things of God.

How do we live as kingdom citizens walking in the eternal realm on earth? We must recognize that if anything ungodly or unrighteous enters our minds, we've stepped out of the realm of eternity. That's our boundary.

Get back into that eternal realm of faith in your mind. If your mind wanders away from that, it's trying to take you back to who you're not. You must get in line with who you are now as a kingdom citizen.

When we talk about walking as a citizen of heaven, it means single-mindedness and not what I'll call "feeling-mindedness." Our unsanctified feelings can get us in a heap of trouble if the way we view the world is lack all the time.

This is a training process just as the military trains for battle. They repeat exercises until they can recognize the enemy no matter what. We, the people of God, must be so well equipped that we recognize the difference between heavenly and earthly things. We must watch ourselves and not engage in earthly things that can impair our kingdom mindsets, because we're not citizens of the earthly realm; we're citizens of heaven.

That word *mind* is broken down to *phrasso*, which means to fence in or enclose, to block up.[5] When we talk about walking as citizens of heaven, we're saying we need to see the kingdom made manifest. We need strong boundaries where our mental faculties focus on this realm of heaven while we walk on earth. We need a mind that is transformed by the truth that Jesus redeemed us, spirit, soul, and body.

Jesus was able to manifest the kingdom not because He was the Son of God but because of His obedience to the Father. He knew where He was seated, in heavenly places by faith. Remember He was in heaven first before He entered our earth time realm. He knew these truths about eternity, even though He walked the earth and had not even died, resurrected, or ascended when He did His biggest miracles. His relationship with the Father was pure and holy, and this relationship kept the veil of the earthly realm away from Him as He performed signs, miracles, and wonders. He has done the same for us but even more so. Because of what He did through His sacrifice, the dominion of death in the earthly realm is defeated. We have even more power. Jesus never got tripped up when people questioned Him or said things to bring confusion or stop the good works He was doing. He maintained the function of walking as a member of heaven on earth through it all.

We're required to do the same thing. Why? Because we're seated with Him in heavenly places. Technically, He's already lifted the church up. Our view is so earthly, but the veil that separates heaven and earth has been removed. Through an open heavenly portal, you can see that what you're doing in this earth realm is connected to the eternal realm of heaven.

I know you have ideas about what you think heaven is, and they are probably based on certain things we read in Scripture. There are specific examples of the throne of God and the sea of

controlled, disciplined, single-vision minds focused on heavenly things first.

IMPARTATION FOR WALKING AS CITIZENS OF HEAVEN

If God is calling you to be trained, to walk as a citizen of heaven, it means things must change. Agree with me as we pray for you to receive an impartation.

> *Father, we thank You that You're teaching us to walk as citizens of heaven and as a community of kingdom citizens in a conversation. Father, I ask for an impartation from this teaching. I ask for a greater revelation of these kingdom royalty truths.*
>
> *Father, You have promoted us into walking as citizens of the kingdom because we have taken our heavenly seats with Jesus. He is ascended and knew how to walk in the earthly realm with power, and He wants us to also. Quicken us to walk in the heavenly realm here on earth, and teach us to practice being single-minded in Jesus' name. Amen.*

EXERCISE IN FAITH

Now that you prayed that prayer, I will ask you to cross an imaginary line in your home and become a citizen of heaven in thought, word, and deed. Just get out of your chair and make an imaginary line in front of you. Then I want you to renounce your earthly citizenship. Tell the Lord you know from Philippians 3:20 that you are a kingdom citizen because of what Jesus did by dying, resurrecting, and ascending, and you want to live this out daily. After you cross the line, jump up and down and say hallelujah! You are now a committed citizen of heaven! You became one when you received Jesus as Lord and Savior. This is another act of maturity, so we call this a step of faith, a spiritual marker for your future as a growing member of God's kingdom.

QUESTIONS for REFLECTION

1. Do you believe you are a citizen of the kingdom of heaven? If so, explain why.

2. What is the biggest hindrance in your mind to walking as a citizen of heaven on earth?

3. What nugget of revelation would you like to see in later chapters to help this teaching become a part of your daily life?

CHAPTER 8

Walking as Citizens of Heaven, Part 2

I HAD MUCH TO share in the last chapter because being a heavenly citizen is who you are. Remember, in the last chapter you crossed the line and renounced your earthly citizenship. And you said that today you would step into your heavenly citizenship. That was an impartation. In this chapter the Lord is following through with your commitment to walk as a citizen of heaven. He will continue to teach you what this new citizenship is all about.

We should have known and been walking in this new way of living already. This teaching has been in the Word of God since it was written, but God brings revelation from heaven. He spills it out bit by bit as He wants His people to receive it. God is now sharing greater revelation with His people about the importance of walking as heavenly citizens. He's also doing this because He knows that the world right now is in a very desperate spot with overwhelming darkness in many ways. We are getting fed so much craziness and lies through the media. Many other voices that are not His voice are getting our ears.

Great darkness has covered the earth, but not for those who know Jesus as their Lord and Savior. We are the light shining in the darkness. We are the ones God has sent to make the change. There has been darkness over the earth from day one. However, we can see it and feel it now in a way that we have not before. It's at another level. There's a saying: "With new levels come new devils." We need to know and understand how to walk as citizens of heaven to defeat the power of darkness.

A great awakening is coming. Revival is coming to the people of God. The darker things get, the hungrier people are for the Word and salvation. When things are great, people think they don't need Jesus, but when things aren't so great, they're more open to knowing Jesus as Lord and Savior. The earth is ripe for salvation. The earth is ripe for revealing the sons and daughters of God, and for revealing the kingdom of heaven now in the earthly realm. As I said before, it's been this way ever since Jesus walked the earth, and He showed us the kingdom of heaven in His example.

> From that time Jesus began to preach, and to say, Repent:
> for the kingdom of heaven is at hand.
>
> —MATTHEW 4:17

CARRY THE KINGDOM

Our job is to carry that out on earth, and God has given us great revelation about how to do that. We read the Word, but we may not necessarily know how to manifest the specific things that the Lord is asking us to carry out. We must manifest a level of confidence that we're supposed to be walking in as kingdom citizens. God continues to reveal more to His apostles, prophets, evangelists, pastors, and teachers. He is telling these fivefold ministry gift leaders to minister by encouraging, edifying, and properly positioning the whole body to live in the light, no matter what's happening around us. I'm happy to have renounced my earthly citizenship and taken on heavenly citizenship. I'm delighted to know that the Lord has been teaching me exactly how to walk like that. I am blessed to know that I can pour that out on you.

In the previous chapter we discussed the power of the mind. The revelation of walking as a citizen of heaven begins with what our minds are focused on. Then the reality of heaven is revealed while we walk in the earthly realm. Our minds have to be centrally focused on the kingdom of God. Honestly, we need to focus on Jesus and our ascension seat because we're seated with Christ in heavenly places. We need to maneuver certain aspects of earthly life as citizens of heaven, and because of that we must learn a new way of walking. It's not new in the sense that it's been written in the Scriptures, but it is a new revelation from heaven on exactly how to do that.

> Even when we were dead in sins, hath quickened us together with Christ, (by grace ye are saved;) and hath raised us up together, and made us sit together in heavenly places in Christ Jesus.
>
> —EPHESIANS 2:5–6

Think about this for a moment: this Scripture passage does not mean that you literally sit in a seat all the time. Heaven is moving and active. Things are taking place in heaven. When the apostle Paul says we're seated with Christ in heavenly places, he doesn't mean we're stationary. He means we have a unique position in heaven.

PORTAL VIEWPOINT

Our position in Christ is a way of saying that we are positioned to see things in the earthly realm from Christ's viewpoint. There is a heavenly portal that enables us to see ourselves from that seat into the earthly realm. We can operate in this heavenly portal by faith and see work done on earth the way God would have it done.

This viewpoint is different. It's a viewpoint of what heaven is like and how it manifests in the earthly realm. We might say, "Well, heaven's not here on earth. Heaven's there above." But technically heaven's here if you're here because you are a portal or gateway for heaven that has arrived. When Jesus showed up, when He walked the earth, heaven was here and the world got an opportunity to watch what heaven was all about through the actions of Jesus, through the way He responded on earth.

The world is watching us too, and they wonder how much we believe about being a citizen of heaven. How much does it impact our decisions? Do we live differently because we know we're citizens of heaven, or do we ignore it and live normal, earthly lives? We must change our thinking here. If we claim to have citizenship in heaven, then while we're here we need to walk as citizens of heaven.

POSSESSING THE LAND OF PROMISE

I want to take you to an Old Testament scripture that highlights the importance of walking as a citizen of heaven.

Then will the LORD drive out all these nations from before you, and ye shall possess greater nations and mightier than yourselves. Every place whereon the soles of your feet shall tread shall be yours: from the wilderness and Lebanon, from the river, the river Euphrates, even unto the uttermost sea shall your coast be.

—DEUTERONOMY 11:23–24

This word was spoken to the Israelites as they were leaving Egypt and going to the Promised Land. It's speaking about the blessings of the Promised Land, a place that God made like heaven on earth. God had chosen that land, and He brought aspects of heaven into it.

When He yanked the people from Egypt to go to the Promised Land, He wanted to show them aspects of Himself. He wanted to say, "I'm great. I'm good. This is what I'm giving you. And when you can fully grasp this, you will know who I am. You will understand My goodness, My love, My promises, and the greatness I want to give you."

Our heavenly Father is so good. He has so much goodness that He has to give it away. We are the recipients of what He's giving away.

Every place whereon the soles of your feet shall tread shall be yours: from the wilderness and Lebanon, from the river, the river Euphrates, even unto the uttermost sea shall your coast be.

—DEUTERONOMY 11:24

God encouraged the Hebrew people that He had a very special place for them, and He would drive out whoever was living in that place currently and bring them into that place. They were empowered by God's promise that everywhere the soles of their feet stepped, they could have that land.

This passage refers to a journey or possession of land during a period of time. In other words, they are called to walk out what they are to possess in the fullness of time, a possession in which nothing is missing and nothing is broken. When it comes to learning how to be a citizen of heaven, we must understand the Hebrew words for soul and feet. God says, "Every place whereon the soles of your feet shall tread shall be yours." The Hebrew word for *sole* is *kaph*, which means the paw of an animal as in power. This word is broken down to *kaphaph*, which means to bow down.[1] This means they will possess when they humble themselves by God's mighty power.

The Hebrew word for *feet* is *regel*, which means to endure as in possessing time.[2] God is saying, "Listen, everywhere you walk, you will possess in humility by My power, and you will even possess time." In other words, you don't need to be concerned about rushing or going too slow. "In My timing," the Lord says, "you're stepping, you're enduring, you're walking in this new place by My power. You're bringing eternal time into earth time and possessing the land." God is redeeming time as you walk!

The Hebrew word for *tread* is *darak*, which means archers hitting the mark.[3] The treading part means that you are hitting the correct mark every time you're moving forward. It means that if anything is under your feet, it's snapped, it's broken. It's been put into a position where it must submit to you. God is saying, "Everywhere the sole of your foot treads, everywhere your feet go, you are taking that land for the kingdom of heaven—for the kingdom of God." This is how powerful we are, and we don't even realize it. This was first spoken to Moses and the Israelites. And this same word was spoken again to Joshua.

> Moses my servant is dead; now therefore arise, go over this Jordan, thou, and all this people, unto the land which I do give to them, even to the children of Israel. Every place that the sole of your foot shall tread upon, that have I given unto you, as I said unto Moses.
>
> —JOSHUA 1:2–3

God repeats that when your walk and focus are on being a citizen of heaven, you take the land with your feet. You stake a spiritual claim that the land is whole, and every demonic force that claims something is missing or broken is lying. We often forget to walk in kingdom power, so we walk as weak ones who lack everything. But when we choose to tread as kingdom citizens and live redeemed, we say poverty is broken, and prosperity, increase, and multiplication have arrived. To recap, when you arrive, all the blessings of the kingdom arrive with you.

Why would God be so specific as to say this in two distinct places in the Old Testament? God knew the people were consumed with fear, lack, and poverty. They had been yanked from the poverty of Egypt to move into the abundance of the Promised Land.

In Egypt they had walked in constant submission to their adverse circumstances, and instead of taking authority they submitted to what was underneath their feet every time they walked. They submitted as slaves in Egypt, not as rulers of a kingdom. This is why God told them specifically, "I'm going to take you from Egypt, and I'm going to take you to the promised land" (Deut. 11:29).

You must know that when you walk, you are enduring. You're on a journey where you possess even unto time. In other words, He's saying, "There's a shift happening between Egypt and the

Promised Land, and this shift is so great that you will need to walk in this level of confidence. You will need to have this level of authority. You will need to know that you're not a citizen of the earth but a citizen of heaven." No matter the trauma you have been through, God will take you from the slavery and demonic oppression of Egypt to the freedom of the Promised Land as you keep treading. I believe right now God is speaking to you about your own circumstances where you feel defeated and overrun by the enemy. He says, "Keep on treading in My power, as I have redeemed the time."

TREAD AS A CITIZEN OF HEAVEN

The enemy claims territory, and God challenges the claim, but He uses us to do that with our delegated authority. God told Satan, "This is not your land. I will send My people with My power. I will increase their faith. I will cause them to start using their feet to take the land that I want to give them. The only thing that stops My people is if they don't believe that everywhere the sole of their foot treads, I've already given them. If they don't have faith in My Word, they won't be walking as heavenly citizens, which means they won't be possessing what they're stepping into."

When we talk about our daily life, use this analogy to put it in perspective: you are overcoming the land everywhere you walk. The enemy has been defeated. You are 100 percent victorious. You have every resource available to you in those two words: *foot* and *tread*. You will possess everywhere you walk, and no matter the journey you take, no matter where you go, you will possess. It also means that you will hit the mark every time you do it, which means if there are snakes and scorpions at your feet, you're killing them along the way.

We're called to walk purposefully. If you don't know your identity as a citizen of heaven, how will you walk with purpose? You might walk with the attitude that says, "Maybe God wants to give it to me. It's a possibility. You know, I've seen Him do things, but not for me." Listen, that's no foot treading! You are called to tread on snakes and scorpions.

We must begin to walk confidently, walk with power, walk straight up. We must walk knowing that we have already obtained what God said, or He would not have said He wants to give it to us. Now, the enemy likes to tell us all these lies while we're walking, but we're not supposed to listen to him. We need to cut off the enemy's voice. You can do this if you realize you're a citizen of heaven because you know that Satan does not reside in the third heaven. If he does not live there, how will he be able to talk to you? This is where you are by faith when you are treading.

When you think, "Well, maybe God wants this for me; I don't know," you've opened yourself up to hear the enemy's voice louder than the voice of God. It's easy to hear God's voice when you walk confidently as a citizen of heaven because you know what the Word says, you stand on the Word, and you know that everywhere your foot goes, you're hitting the mark. Just as an archer takes his bow and hits his target, you know that you're purposeful.

God wanted the Israelites to have this kind of attitude when they left Egypt and headed for the Promised Land. Now, granted, He told them what He wanted them to be, but it took them a long journey to turn into those people. There are other things I'll show you in future chapters that God did for them on the journey that proved they were walking as citizens of heaven. Even at that time, everything God had spoken to them would indeed come to pass.

When we have doubt and fear, we miss the best part of being

with God while we're taking the land He's calling us to see. We all enjoy the sweetest fellowship with God when we know what He's called us to do, that He's given us the power to do it, and that we can commune with Him while we're taking the land. We need to preserve that. The enemy robs us of that when God orders us to do something, but we murmur and complain or live in fear and lack. We're being robbed of our moment with God while we're taking the very land He asked us to possess. Then when we finally make it, we say, "Oh my goodness, I made it! Why did I spend the entire time in doubt and fear?" And we're upset with ourselves because God was faithful to His word.

It's much better to live as citizens right away and say, "Listen, my God will be true to His word. I will walk this thing out no matter what. We will get ourselves to the promised land." Each time we walk, we hit that mark and our feet cause us to possess in that particular moment. It's much better to be that way because we will enjoy the journey instead of complaining during it. Portals that open the glory realm to the earth will open when we endeavor to live like this because we are living as a redeemed people. You have a responsibility as a citizen of heaven to learn to walk like this.

> For we are his workmanship, created in Christ Jesus unto good works, which God hath before ordained that we should walk in them.
>
> —Ephesians 2:10

The Greek word for *walk* is *peripateo*, which means to tread all around as proof of the ability to deport oneself.[4] It also is broken down into two other Greek words. The first is *peri*, which means to have respect for a place, cause, or time.[5] It means there is a circumstance, a matter, or a general period of time to circuit around, access beyond, or complete through. The other Greek word is *pateo*, which means to trample or tread under foot.[6] In other words, *peripateo* means when you're walking, you're walking with the ability that everything is already complete as though in a circuit or circle of time and you are possessing what is under your feet. Time is redeemed in a circle of completeness.

ETERNAL TIME MEETS EARTH TIME

Can you imagine walking with this extraordinary ability and everything already being complete? It's already finished. It's already done. This is the power of that word *peripateo*. It means circular time or running like a circuit. A circuit means a point that starts and goes to the other end like a circle. A circle is never-ending; it's complete. This means that everywhere you walk the sole of your foot is hitting the mark in completeness, and wholeness is taking place—nothing missing, nothing broken. You even possess earthly time in the middle of it, which means that *God ordained works for you to do in the eternal realm before any one of those works came to be in the earthly realm you now walk in.* In other words, it was written that you would walk and complete the assignment God had given you before you ever trod it out. Why? Because you are His workmanship, called to good works that God prepared for you to do. He prepared those good works in advance from the eternal realm. Then why do we walk in fear, doubt, discouragement, and worry? If it's already complete, it's been done, and it's been written, then you have already succeeded as you begin walking.

Listen to the component of time in this. As I shared in previous chapters, time is different to us in the earthly realm than it is in the heavenly realm. When we're walking as citizens of heaven, we debunk time because it is redeemed from the curse. We open portals of time that release the eternal into the earth. There is eternal time and then earthly time. Heaven or the eternal is timeless. It's all timeless from beginning to end because God created the earth in the beginning.

The Greek word for *beginning* is *alpha*, and the end is *omega*. Jesus is the Alpha and Omega, the beginning and the end (Rev. 1:8). If everything is Him, and in Him, and every work was already written before time, then our job is to tread with confidence that we're hitting every mark, and this is already complete from an eternal realm perspective. Therefore, success has already been had. It's a past thing. It's already been taken care of. Your success was already finished before you even started walking. Redemption occurred because of Jesus' death, resurrection, and ascension, so time is complete. Let me say that again: *your success was finished before you even started walking.* That's powerful.

I spent time explaining the Greek words used in this passage because they help us see that He's already had the power and authority to debunk every evil force coming against everything we're doing. Your situation is already overcome as you begin walking. Everything you happen to be going through at this moment, no matter how severe, is overcome and redeemed. You've already succeeded in every single moment before any one of them came to be.

Here's what's so powerful about this. The Lord spoke this to me in an audible voice. He said, "Candice, everywhere I send you, the work is already done."

I asked, "Lord, then why am I all concerned about that thing I'm about ready to do?"

He said, "I don't know. Candice, why are you concerned about that? Because it's already been done. It's already been written, and there's already been a successful outcome from the eternal heavenly realm. Candice, a portal was open, and you are now walking on earth time, but this was a success in the eternal heavenly time zone. Will you enjoy the moment and start walking until you get to your destination? And then I will give you another order about what the next steps are."

That's living in heaven on earth. Redemption has occurred. It should ease your pain. If you can meditate on this all day while you're going about your daily life, you will have the greatest joy. You will not be trying to impress your boss. You will not be trying to work hard for approval. You will not do all these earthly things that you have been trained to do as you conform to the pattern of the world. Instead you will step into a place where your mind is now transformed. You will say, "Well, I can simply enjoy this because I know it will be a success. I have the victory! It's already written, and I am just walking it out." I share additional teaching on this in my book *Soul Transformation*.[7]

THE WORD STATES ETERNAL TIME FIRST

> In the beginning was the Word, and the Word was with God, and the Word was God. The same was in the beginning with God.
>
> —JOHN 1:1–2

Jesus walked the earth. He was the Word. Everything that God does succeeds. He wrote His Word in the eternal realm and manifested it through a portal to show His success on earth from heaven's perspective. Because time was redeemed, even when people are having their worst times they are not defeated.

Everything about this good word is a success from page one to the end. It's the story of victory that has already been completed and done from the only real-time perspective, which is eternal. God is the victorious one, and He wrote it for us to know how victorious He is. Again, real time is eternal time, not earthly time. Earthly time lags behind eternal time.

Many people say, "We win in the end." You may have heard someone hold up their Bible and say, "I read the Book of Revelation, and we win in the end." Eternal time is being stated in a written word about when earth time manifests it. In other words, it is a true statement from an earthly time perspective. But from heaven's perspective, we don't only win in the end, we win now in the present time. We've already won from eternity. The story was already written; it is past tense. Time has been redeemed.

You are in this moment today, and you win in this next minute. You win in the next minute and the next. You won when it was written in the eternal realm, and now you are walking it out in the earthly realm.

Eternal time has more power than earth time. Earth time must submit to eternal time just as we and the world must submit to God and His time and season for everything. The word written in advance is about good works that we carry out now in the earthly realm. This eternal portal gives peace to the earthly moment. It is a real portal that opens us up in the eternal realm but is made manifest in the present earthly realm. It is where you get on an eternal time clock instead of an earthly one, and you begin to rest in time because it was redeemed by Jesus, instead of race in time for fear it will die.

When we look at it this way, as citizens of heaven, what are we upset about? The story of the Israelites coming from Egypt to the Promised Land is a written story of the Lord revealing who

He is and who His Son, Jesus, is to a specific group of people He chose to tell His story to. God had to show us through the Jewish people how He worked with humans stuck in earthly time. The story of the Israelites reveals that God is the lifesaver who took a group of people from their earthly understanding to eternal understanding.

The Lord revealed the Israelites' journey, and in doing so He revealed His nature of love and goodness to us all. He showed us through them how He would work the eternal truths out of our heavenly Garden of Eden into the earthly realm since the enemy had robbed us of time in our earthly Garden of Eden. The enemy put us in a realm of lack and poverty. Humanity was subjected to earthly time when all along it should have been on the time zone of heaven, which is eternal. Death robbed us and time was cut short when Adam and Eve ate the forbidden fruit. But Jesus bought back time and made it eternal, and now those who believe in Him as Savior will never die separated from God. And by the power of the Holy Spirit, a portal is open where we can now walk as citizens of heaven.

All along, this timeline was earthly for us but not for God. He was in the eternal time zone all along, and His days were alpha to omega, beginning to end. Again, earthly time exists because the enemy stopped eternal time when Adam and Eve sinned, and they got us stuck in this earthly time zone of death where we would lose everlasting life. But God knew better, and He revealed the system of redemption in the garden when He made animal skins for Adam and Eve and placed a flaming sword as a guard when He kicked them out (Gen. 3:24). There was one way back home to the eternal realm. The portal would be open again when Jesus fulfilled the covenant and died, resurrected, and ascended. Then the dominion of death would be broken, and we could enter the eternal time zone again. Redemption of time would occur even at the flaming sword in the garden.

THE ETERNAL PORTAL IS OPEN EVERY DAY

When we choose Jesus as our Lord and Savior, redemption takes place and we enter the portal of eternal life. You should remember the day you got saved or entered the eternal time zone and Ephesians 2:10 became your motto. You know the day of your natural birth. Do you know the day you were born in the eternal realm? It's your day of salvation, the day when you believed Jesus as your Lord, Savior, and Messiah.

Jesus talked to Nicodemus about this.

> Jesus answered and said unto him, Verily, verily, I say unto thee, Except a man be born again, he cannot see the kingdom of God. Nicodemus saith unto him, How can a man be born when he is old? can he enter the second time into his mother's womb, and be born? Jesus answered, Verily, verily, I say unto thee, Except a man be born of water and of the Spirit, he cannot enter into the kingdom of God. That which is born of the flesh is flesh; and that which is born of the Spirit is spirit. Marvel not that I said unto thee, Ye must be born again.
>
> —John 3:3–7

Jesus referred to the day we entered the portal of eternal life. He was the doorway to this realm. You may be celebrating your natural or spiritual birthday today. Happy birthday to you from an earth perspective and an eternal one. You had to be able to track your natural birth. And you should know how to track when you got saved and entered into the eternal realm as one born-again in the spirit. This spiritual birth into the eternal heavenly realm takes a lot of learning and understanding on how to walk in the heavenly realm on earth. This is the kingdom citizen teaching that you have been reading in this book. Before your spiritual birth into the eternal realm, you were already written in heaven—your whole story already told—and guess what? You're a success. You are a success now every day, giving you a real reason to have joy.

> My substance was not hid from thee, when I was made in secret, and curiously wrought in the lowest parts of the earth. Thine eyes did see my substance, yet being unperfect; and in thy book all my members were written, which in continuance were fashioned, when as yet there was none of them.
>
> —PSALM 139:15–16

All the days of our lives were written before anyone came to be. In other words, your redemption of every life choice was written when you accepted Jesus as your Lord and Savior. These are the good works written from an eternal heavenly realm that exists in every moment of our lives. We carry that truth out every day we live on earth. See the time component again. Eternal surpasses earthly, so if you shift your soul in the present to eternal time while you walk in the earthly realm, how much more peace will you have? Oh, so much more, and you will stop trying to save time and start enjoying it.

In Philippians 4:3 the apostle Paul is talking about those who served with him, and he says,

> And I intreat thee also, true yokefellow, help those women which laboured with me in the gospel, with Clement also,

and with other my fellowlabourers, whose names are in the book of life.

It is called the Book of Life because those who have believed in Jesus have entered the portal of eternal life, and now you have a word written about you. It is proof that at the end of your earthly life you will live on eternally.

The last scripture I want to share with you in this chapter is Luke 10:19–20, as Jesus spoke to His disciples.

> Behold, I give unto you power to tread on serpents and scorpions, and over all the power of the enemy: and nothing shall by any means hurt you. Notwithstanding in this rejoice not, that the spirits are subject unto you; but rather rejoice, because your names are written in heaven.

He told them in the Old Testament books of Deuteronomy and Joshua, everywhere the sole of your foot treads, you have taken this land. You've hit every mark in possession of time. And then Jesus shows up on the scene, and He tells the disciples, "I have given you the power to tread on serpents and scorpions, because anywhere you walk, whatever you are doing, you're walking in the earthly realm, and you're walking on whatever is under your feet." Why is it under your feet? Because Jesus was saying, "You're already seated with Me in heavenly places."

When Jesus came to earth, and He went through His terrible death and shed His blood, He already knew He would be a success. Every time He spoke the Word, He was saying, "Listen to me; I'm teaching you the Word of God. I am telling you what was already done from the foundation of the world. I am redemption of the curse. And it's all about My redeeming you and properly positioning you."

Every time you open the Word of God, He's wooing you. He's saying, "I know you think this is too good to be true. It's not too good to be true. Everything I've said is the truth. It will come to pass, and you will be victorious in every way. All your time from your natural birth to your natural physical death is just a dash in the eternal realm. Don't rush through your life." Don't rush through your life because He's with you in the earthly realm. And He wants to be with you in the middle of it. He wants you to experience His joy.

He wants you to know His goodness and greatness. You should have joy every day of your life because everywhere He sent you, you've already been in a successful place that was written from the eternal heavenly perspective. Don't rush yourself, but stay right where you are and fill your heart with the immense joy of knowing time has been made complete. He's giving you a piece of heaven on earth. He says, "Rise and walk as a citizen of heaven. Here's a piece of heaven. You are redeemed. Every day in your past is redeemed, and every day in your present and future is redeemed." He's a great God. He's an awesome King. He's a victorious God, and He has made each of us victorious already.

PRAYER OF FAITH

We thank You, Father, because everywhere our foot treads we are stepping into the promises of how great You are. We have joy in our lives because we can walk with You in Your greatness. We can revel in You. We can enjoy You on the journey. We don't have to hate this moment, no matter how bad it is. It is a redeemed moment in time. It's just part of the journey because we're already successful. Everything about our lives is victorious, and we will not be concerned about earthly time every day that we walk. It's already been written from eternal time. Jesus gave it to us, Father. We praise and thank You today. We will enjoy the life You gave us and walk as citizens of heaven. Because of everything Jesus did, we can have victory in every area.

Father God, thank You so much for what Your Son, Jesus, did. His sacrifice brought us eternal life and opened the portals of heaven and the eternal realm. Thank You that He agreed to redeem us. We get to be part of that redemption, and we give You glory, honor, and praise. Lord, activate our senses as we step into the reality of knowing that everything is made perfect in eternal time. Help us walk daily from this benefit that came when Jesus died, resurrected, and ascended and we as the church became seated with Him in heavenly places now active to walk this earth. Thank You, Jesus! Amen.

QUESTIONS for REFLECTION

1. How does it feel to know that everywhere your foot treads you have completed an element of earthly time, and it is redeemed?

2. How will you work this revelation out in your daily life? What is God bringing to your mind?

3. Do you understand the power of what Jesus did when He shifted us from earthly time to eternal time when we received salvation? What does this mean for you personally?

CHAPTER 9

Kingdom Treading

ON THE LAST chapter I shared that everywhere your foot treads you have the authority to trample on snakes and scorpions. You are taking that land. Joshua was ready to lead the people to dispossess nations and step into the Promised Land after forty years in the desert.

> Moses my servant is dead; now therefore arise, go over this Jordan, thou, and all this people, unto the land which I do give to them, even to the children of Israel. Every place that the sole of your foot shall tread upon, that have I given unto you, as I said unto Moses.
>
> —JOSHUA 1:2–3

If you remember from the last chapter, the Hebrew word for *foot* is *regel*. It means to step, endure, journey, and possess time. It means to walk along and possess time. It means to move on the journey, and each step of the way you possess the land God gives you. This possessing of land is from an eternal heavenly perspective. You are redeeming the curse of time as you walk. The eternal perspective means you are bringing the activities that take place in earth time into fullness and completeness. You walk on earth from the heavenly perspective that you are a citizen of heaven seated with Christ in heavenly places. You tread along, and everywhere your foot steps you are possessing eternally. The present realm belongs to you because of what Jesus did. You're hitting the mark with your tread.

In other words as you step, the curse, which is anything that's under your feet, is being suppressed. This curse has no power with every step you're taking. You now possess the land, and you're doing it in a way that means the enemy has no ground. You have all the ground, so when we talk about treading on the land, we talk about striking the ground with our feet. We are redeeming the time with the power of what Jesus accomplished to raise us to be seated with Him. We talk about single blows and striking the way an archer takes the bow and hits the target. You're striking anything that's underneath your feet. Think about this from a demonic perspective. If we're seated with Christ in heavenly places, demonic forces are underneath us right now. Since you're walking in the heavenly realm on earth, you are walking as if you're in an eternal heavenly bubble.

GOD KNEW IN ETERNAL TIME

Remember, all this has already been taken care of since the beginning of time when Jesus, the Father, and the Holy Spirit decided that Jesus would come to earth and die for our sins, shed His blood, resurrect, and ascend. In Genesis God refers to more than just Him in the existence of eternal time.

> God said, "Let us make man in our image, after our likeness: and let them have dominion over the fish of the sea, and over the fowl of the air, and over the cattle, and over all the earth, and over every creeping thing that creepeth upon earth."
>
> —GENESIS 1:26

The *us* is God, Jesus, and the Holy Spirit; They decided these things. They foreknew that sin would enter the world, and it would have to be corrected. They knew sin would bring an eternal death that would affect the realm of earthly time.

As we tread we live out His victory on earth—what's already taken place in the eternal realm as completion of Jesus' finished work on the cross, His resurrection, and His ascension. Demonic forces may appear to be at the same level as you in the first heaven. But they are not because you're in the third-heaven level in the eternal realm by faith. You may see yourself as living on earth, but God sees you as seated with Him in heavenly places. You must have full knowledge of this truth in your soul, that indeed you're there. Then you must keep yourself there from a mental and soul standpoint. We can't get all flaky and go back and forth between earth and heaven. Either we are people who walk in power and tread on snakes and scorpions because of our seated position with Christ, or we don't believe what the apostle Paul tells us in Ephesians 2:6. People with power don't question who they are. They know their true identity, and all decisions flow from this. Doubt brings about double-mindedness. We must be single-minded to rule as citizens of heaven.

Remember our caped crusader superhero named Superman, who was earthly Clark Kent, as he watched for evil to come into the earth so he could then activate who he really was, which was Superman. He just looked earthly, but he wasn't; he was superhuman.

You might have an earthly appearance. You may be in an earth suit and an earth body, but essentially you're spiritual and supernatural. You are spirit first and flesh second. When we talk about the heavenly realm, we must walk in the confidence that we're walking heavenly everywhere we go, even though we're on earth. Evil forces may aggravate, but generally they will stay at bay, and they can't touch you. If you allow them to aggravate you, that's your freewill choice. In essence you can just say to the demonic forces, "Talk to the hand. I don't see you. I don't hear you. I don't want anything to do with you."

You must stay consistent in the fight. Our free will causes us to be entrapped and ensnared by the aggravation demons bring us. We can stand fast in the faith, walking in this eternal portal or eternal bubble. If you can imagine it, this eternal bubble would be, from center to circumference, like a legitimate spot of heaven that surrounds you, but it's on earth. It can operate doing everything just as heaven would operate. To live like this, you must change your thinking. The only way for that to happen is to get into the Word of God. The Bible will transform your mind until you begin to believe who you really are and live in this heavenly portal on earth. Remember, redemption bought all of this for you.

To walk in this power, though, you must continue to wash in the Word. You must believe you're a spiritual being, not only because of the power of God within you but also because of a realm in which you operate that comes from an open heavenly portal surrounding you. That realm has all the power of heaven. It is a kingdom realm.

The kingdom realm is like a bubble of protection around you

all the time. It's as though there's an open portal from heaven. It goes everywhere with you. You might see and touch things in the natural, but it doesn't matter because that heavenly bubble is where all the power lies.

Inside this heavenly bubble is only eternal time. This is where you defy earthly time. Defying earthly time is a blessing of walking in the eternal realm on earth. It will open heaven so that the glory is released in the earthly realm. You need to quicken an understanding of that portal and how to enter it and stay in it.

As I have mentioned in previous chapters, we got into this mess because Adam and Eve had a dialogue with the serpent in the garden instead of using their authority and saying, "Talk to the hand, devil." We are the product of the generations of sin that came from the seed of Adam and Eve.

> And the LORD God said unto the serpent, Because thou hast done this, thou art cursed above all cattle, and above every beast of the field; upon thy belly shalt thou go, and dust shalt thou eat all the days of thy life: And I will put enmity between thee and the woman, and between thy seed and her seed; it shall bruise thy head, and thou shalt bruise his heel.
>
> —GENESIS 3:14–15

Look at what God did when He cursed Satan: He automatically put him under our feet. Satan doesn't get to be a flying creature. He's cursed on the ground already, cursed to slither there, which means you're higher than him, right away. Then the curse continues by the Lord. God says, "All right, serpent, I will put enmity [hatred] between you and the woman, and between your seed and her seed, and her seed will bruise your head, and you shall bruise his heel." This means there is a division between the children of God, the called ones of God, and the demonic. There's a difference. God says, "I'm creating this division. You all are not alike. You're not close; you're separate."

Then God says, "And I'm giving Jesus and the born-again humans redemptive power, and this is what will happen. They will bruise your head. In other words, Satan, they will stomp on you because you're cursed, and they will have the redemptive power because you, serpent, will bruise the heel of King Jesus."

When Jesus hung on the cross, He had nails in His hands and feet. He was bruised in His feet. Jesus' death on the cross gives us the power of redemption. We were born into the natural earthly realm because of Eve. And Jesus was also born through that holy line. He became the seed of the woman that did the job on the cross to crush the enemy's head. I need you to think about that for a second.

I don't know why we get so upset about demonic forces when they don't have any power. They were stripped of that in Genesis 3, but we give them power because we believe in what they can do and how they can destroy. If you don't give them power, you will always overcome them from the heavenly portal.

When we are born, we enter the world struggling, and we keep struggling. By the age of twelve, which theologians say is the age of reason, we begin to recognize that not only do we do things wrong, but that something is missing and broken—that we are not whole. We begin to understand that we need a Savior when we get to a level of conscious recognition. If we're invited to know Jesus and what He has done for us, that's when things start turning around. We begin to fight against our stinking "world thinking" acquired since natural birth. We begin to establish a true identity of who we are. We begin to understand we are redeemed from the curse of sin, death, and the grave because of what Jesus did.

In Genesis 3 God said, "Listen, I put Satan down there, and I crushed him. And all My kids must do is keep walking, keep treading, and they will walk on snakes and scorpions and overpower them." He took care of our issues through Jesus' sacrifice.

THE LORD'S PRAYER FOR KINGDOM ON EARTH

Fast-forward to the New Testament, where Jesus is teaching His disciples how to pray.

> After this manner therefore pray ye: Our Father which art in heaven, Hallowed be thy name. Thy kingdom come, Thy will be done in earth, as it is in heaven. Give us this day our daily bread. And forgive us our debts, as we forgive our debtors. And lead us not into temptation, but deliver us from evil: For thine is the kingdom, and the power, and the glory, for ever. Amen.
>
> —MATTHEW 6:9–13

Jesus told them to pray that prayer because that's how His kingdom operates. If we stay within the boundaries of the Lord's Prayer, we will enter the heavenly kingdom portal and walk in this realm on earth. When Jesus died and resurrected, He overcame sin, death, and the grave.

Yet, remember in John 20:17, right before He ascended, He spoke to Mary: "Listen, don't cling to me, Mary. I haven't yet gone to My Father and your Father." In other words, "What I did makes us one with the Father." He's our Father because His Son, Jesus Christ, gave His life so that He could reconcile us to the Father.

We can live in the kingdom now in earthly time. Jesus is saying to His disciples, "I want you to live as though the kingdom has already come; it has been redeemed. I want you to pray, 'Thy kingdom come, Thy will be done, on earth as it is in heaven.'" Why would Jesus ask us to pray that prayer if it were impossible to have the kingdom come to earth now?

Prayers are affirmations of truth. We pray what we already know is true. We pray the will of the Father, and it shall be done. It's already God's will that the kingdom come to the earth because He sent Jesus. Jesus told the disciples to pray a prayer of God's heart and God's redemptive power through Him. We don't pray what's not possible. We only pray what is possible because we know God will meet us by faith. We carry the truth of the eternal heavenly kingdom in our prayers, and then we succeed in our prayer life. When you ask it, you receive it by faith because of God's goodness.

> Ask, and it shall be given you; seek, and ye shall find; knock, and it shall be opened unto you: For every one that asketh receiveth; and he that seeketh findeth; and to him that knocketh it shall be opened.
> —MATTHEW 7:7–8

Let's look at the differences in the Lord's Prayer between "in earth" and "in heaven." When we pray that "it will be done on earth as it is in heaven," we're saying that we want superimposition of time, place, and order. We want a distribution over, above, and in the direction of God's will. When we say we want things to happen "in earth as it is in heaven," we're saying we want heaven to rest on earth. When that happens, heaven's time, place, and order become a reality in the earthly realm. That's what we're praying.

When we say we want this on earth as it is in heaven, we are asking that the state of heaven, which is the state of eternal time and rest, would come to the earth. We are asking the Lord to let the peace and rest of heaven come to earth. In other words, "Lord, superimpose the rest of heaven on the chaos that surrounds us. I want heaven to rule over the earth." It is possible because Jesus redeemed the time.

He made a way for that to happen because you are in a portal or bubble in which heaven already exists. Remember that wherever you are, the eternal heavenly portal is open and heaven is right there. Jesus made a door in which your beliefs are now being made manifest on earth. This portal of the heavenly realm touches the earth realm. If we act in faith that the kingdom has arrived, we're living out what we asked in the Lord's Prayer. We're living out our belief that heaven has superimposed our present earthly time, the earthly order, the earthly rank, anything on earth. Heaven has come upon it.

If you're asking for that, you better know what you're asking for. Jesus wanted His followers to pray this prayer, and He hadn't even died yet. He says, "Pray this because this is the will of My Father, and I know I will go to the cross. I will shed My blood. I will resurrect and ascend. Then I will send you the Holy Spirit." Jesus talked about what He knew to be true, and it was true. This enables us to live in the heavenly portal, because time is redeemed.

HEAVEN SUPERIMPOSES EARTH

Before the Israelites went into the Promised Land, they had to wander the desert for forty years. This great release from the bondage of Egypt came with God revealing His power in a pillar of cloud by day and fire by night, the miracle of crossing the Red Sea, and the power of standing and being delivered supernaturally. The Israelites were set free, then they got on the other side, and it took them quite a while to get to the land of Canaan, called the Promised Land. They even murmured and complained along the way and started asking to go back to Egypt after seeing that the journey would be difficult.

Here's the thing I want you to grasp. Before the Israelites entered the Promised Land, they saw heaven superimpose the earthly realm while traveling in the desert for forty years. It blows me away to realize that they murmured and complained to go back, yet they were in a heavenly portal or realm where the miracles of God were manifest. Miracles redeem time because they break the curse of sin, death, and the grave. Let me tell you how I know they were in the heavenly realm.

> And thou shalt remember all the way which the LORD thy God led thee these forty years in the wilderness, to humble thee, and to prove thee, to know what was in thine heart, whether thou wouldest keep his commandments, or no.
>
> And he humbled thee, and suffered thee to hunger, and fed thee with manna, which thou knewest not, neither did thy fathers know; that he might make thee know that man doth not live by bread only, but by every word that proceedeth out of the mouth of the LORD doth man live.
>
> Thy raiment waxed not old upon thee, neither did thy foot swell, these forty years.
>
> —DEUTERONOMY 8:2–4

These were truths from heaven realized in the desert before going into the Promised Land. It says specifically that the Lord fed them manna every day. They couldn't even take more of the manna. Once they saw it, they only had enough for one day. It was perfect. It was crushed coriander seed. It was baked like a honey cracker. We talk about superfoods. Well, this was a superfood straight from heaven. They got manna from heaven.

It says that their clothing did not wear out, and their feet did not swell for forty years. If you're like me, your feet swell when you've only walked an hour. Most clothing wears out in a few years. But it says no clothing wore out, their feet had no swelling, and they were fed bread from heaven every day. They were walking in the heavenly realm on earth.

Manna represents the bread of life, which is Jesus. They eat this manna every day. Their feet are not swelling, and their clothes are not wearing out. The word *clothes* means mantle. Their mantle, as in who they are—their calling—is not wearing out. This meant they did not worry about their covering, as He would keep it clean and laundered and not decaying.

Their feet did not swell. Again, remember that the Hebrew word for *foot* is *regel*, meaning to endure, journey, and possess time. Their feet were possessing time. Every single moment they were living, possessing the land God called them to. Swelling is a type of decay. No swelling means there was no decay. This means total life was with them even when they complained, but they did not recognize it because they had too much of Egypt inside them. God was trying to get Egypt—its memory and bondage to idols—out of them. Egypt was a reminder of the pain of the earthly realm, the pain of the fall of humanity.

Today many still have a lot of Egypt inside. These earthly things in our souls make it difficult for us to walk in the heavenly realm on earth. God has given it to us, and by faith we can see it, smell it, taste it, touch it, and believe it. The Word of God says that heaven should be superimposed on earth now, not later. Redemption has taken place.

The same goes for us today. Your mantle is long-standing, and it is evidence of who you are and what God has called you to do. Your feet have the power to strike evil and crush the enemy daily. Your manna is the superfood you take in every day when you read the Word of God and meditate on it as God told Joshua.

> This book of the law shall not depart out of thy mouth; but thou shalt meditate therein day and night, that thou mayest observe to do according to all that is written therein: for then thou shalt make thy way prosperous, and then thou shalt have good success. Have not I commanded thee? Be strong and of a good courage; be not afraid, neither be thou dismayed: for the LORD thy God is with thee whithersoever thou goest.
>
> —JOSHUA 1:8–9

Man is not supposed to live on bread or natural food alone but on every rhema word that comes from the mouth of the Lord; that's the true manna from heaven. Jesus is the bread of life. The true manna, every word that comes forth, is Jesus, as He is the Word! This Word will change you. This Word will transform you into believing that you are walking in heaven on earth.

We must stop talking about things that aren't right and start talking about heaven. No matter what earthly things were happening, Jesus, as our example, always talked the way His Father wanted Him to, which was "kingdom talk" all the time. We need to choose not to use our tongue for earthly things but heavenly things.

Heaven is here right now. We don't have to die and go there. It's here because we're here. The Lord's Prayer says, "May it be done on earth as it is in heaven." There's a superimposing of the eternal onto what is natural and has the appearance of death. But as you know, decay and death have been defeated, so our responsibility is to live today. As we walk on earth, our first test is to understand that the serpent is under our feet.

That happened in Genesis 3. The devil is a serpent and can only go on his belly all the days of his life. Why? God's people had the power because Jesus was their answer to the devil, as His heel was bruised but the enemy's head was crushed. We must renew our minds so we can activate heaven in the earthly realm now, not later, and not only at our death on earth. God needs you now to walk or tread like this with the authority He gave you. Jesus has redeemed the curse of death, which stole our time.

PRAYER OF REPENTANCE FOR EARTHLY SIGHT

I want us to repent of everything we doubt, everything we see negatively. Repent of everything in which you see too much earth and not enough heaven.

> *Father, I need to repent. I thank You right now in the mighty name of Jesus. I repent, Lord, of looking at something and only seeing death or decay. Forgive me for not realizing that You have already supplied life. When the Israelites walked in the wilderness, You supplied all their needs, and there was nothing but life around them. Their feet were full of life. Their clothes or mantles were full of life. The manna or food they got was full of life. Lord, You have my situation under control in every way. Therefore, no matter what death I may see with my natural eyes, You have it under control. I thank You that You're washing me, Father, in Jesus' name.*

FAITH ACTIVATION

Lord, I ask for new eyesight. I want new spiritual eyes to see how I should walk in the heavenly realm on earth. Father, empower me to walk in the heavenly realm by increasing my faith. I ask that You activate my spiritual senses of sight, smell, taste, touch, and hearing so they come alive in the mighty name of Jesus. I need to become aware that You have given me everything I need to supersede the earth and crush the enemy. The curse is broken, and I am called today to live in the heavenly realm.

I thank You for my mantle. I thank You for the bread of life. I thank You for feeding me the Word. Teach me to tread well and take possession of the land, as time has been redeemed. Help me realize that no enemy force can prosper against me because they are under my feet in the eternal heavenly realm and the earthly realm. I give You glory, honor, and praise, and I declare that I am changed in Jesus' name. Amen.

QUESTIONS for REFLECTION

1. Do you understand the power that God has given you to tread on snakes and scorpions?

2. What doubts are you still holding on to about your power in the earthly realm?

3. How will you change your life or thinking as a kingdom citizen to superimpose heaven on earth?

CHAPTER 10

Strategy: You Can Have It

$\mathcal{I}$ WAS A GUEST speaker at a women's event in Oklahoma, and I got a chance to see the portal of heavenly prosperity open up in the church. I have been a part of some financial miracles before, but this one, in my opinion, was jaw-dropping. It was Saturday morning, and they had received an offering for my ministry because I was the guest speaker. Afterward they asked me to start speaking. Well, as soon as I came up, the Holy Spirit said to me, "You will take another offering, but it's for the missions work in this church." And I thought, "Whoa, Lord, I don't usually take offerings while I'm a guest speaker in somebody else's church." This was the internal conversation I had with the Lord. This church does a lot of missions work in Nepal and Paraguay, some of the most challenging parts of the world. I knew I had to do it because I felt the Holy Spirit's deep conviction, and the glory was released.

I asked the ushers to bring the offering buckets. I told the people, "This is an offering for the missions ministry of this church. I want you all to bless the pastors because they have plans for things that they want to do, and this is what the Lord wants." A few people came forward with offerings, and then the ushers took the buckets back. I felt in my spirit they were not supposed to take the buckets away. I said, "No, let's leave the buckets up here. This is a missions offering for them. I want these buckets to stay up here until I finish speaking."

A couple of minutes later a woman in the front row got up, walked to the back of the church, handed an offering to the usher, and left. She had been at the women's conference on Friday night, and she was there Saturday morning until the offering time. We didn't see her on Sunday.

After that Saturday morning service the host pastors came to me in shock. They said, "Oh my, look at this blessing!" They showed me a $10,000 check for their missions work, signed by the woman who had left the service at offering time. They cried and said, "We can now pay for the missions work we want to do in Paraguay and Nepal."

I thought, "Lord, You are so good." He will meet the needs of every ministry. He will take care of who He has called to do His work.

SHIFT THE REALM

It's amazing to assess how we ask God for blessings. We pray "white-knuckle prayers" and beg loudly as though God can't hear or doesn't care. We pray with no faith for things that require so much faith. We say, "Lord, please, please do this or that!" The key is to get yourself into the heavenly portal of prosperity that flows from the vats of heaven, and you will see the eternal realm of wealth that you have been given. You will be able to access this portal of wealth and bring it into the earthly realm because it's already yours in the eternal realm. It's already yours, and you possess this wealth at this time. You possess all that in the eternal realm because of the redemption of time. Our biggest problem is opening the heavenly portal by faith and shifting from the earthly to the eternal.

We must enter the eternal realm and cause it to impact the earthly realm. We must shift ourselves through a portal out of the earthly realm and into the heavenly realm. That's what I want to talk about in this chapter. In other words, if you can see it, you can have it.

If you can see it, you can have it! What does this mean? I've been teaching you that you are called to walk as citizens of heaven on earth. The apostle Paul told us to do this.

> But we are citizens of heaven, where the Lord Jesus Christ lives. And we are eagerly waiting for him to return as our Savior.
>
> —PHILIPPIANS 3:20, NLT

GOOD WORKS DONE FIRST IN HEAVEN

If we are walking in heaven as well as being citizens of heaven walking on earth, then in essence we are treading out the earthly realm with eternal heavenly power. We are making a way here on earth by what has already taken place in heaven.

The apostle Paul says that we're citizens in heaven, and we eagerly await our Savior, the Lord Jesus. As citizens of heaven we are called to walk in the earthly realm as though we are a citizen of heaven. Different blessings come with our ability to walk. As we walk along, thinking about where we're going and what we're doing, we need to remember that we are walking in a pathway already created for us.

> For we are his workmanship, created in Christ Jesus unto good works, which God hath before ordained that we should walk in them.
>
> —EPHESIANS 2:10

In other words, everything we do in the earthly realm—even these moments right now—has already been accomplished and completed in the eternal realm because it is redeemed. The things you do today have already happened somewhere else: in heaven! The works you do were already done somewhere else. Eternal time is finished and complete, and the current time is earthly. We carry out what is technically already done. Everything you think and do was already done in heaven and is now manifesting on earth. Pretty amazing!

Why do we worry? Because we are deceived into believing this earth realm holds the keys to time. It does not. It is a reflection of heaven, which is timeless and complete already. Jesus made a way for us to experience now the benefits of eternal time in the earthly realm. The truth is what you do here was already done there, and it's complete. So when you walk out something here on earth, you are treading out what is already accomplished.

This truth is essential because if it's already been done from the framework of eternity, that means it's already perfect, whole, and complete. Before we do anything we walk by faith in the portal of eternity that holds what's already been done and what is already the will and nature of God. Ephesians 2:10 talks specifically about good works He prepared, which are works suitable for His purpose. Because He is good what comes from Him are good things in the earthly realm. Sometimes it's hard to identify what's good and what's not good.

It's hard for us to know what God is doing in a moment, but we must believe it is good since He is good, and these are His moments on earth we are walking in. We must know and trust that He has ordained these good works because we are connected to Him. We will then bring those good works out into the earthly realm by the power that Jesus made possible to redeem everything and make it like heaven on earth. These statements about heavenly things will manifest on earth.

If you want to be in sync with what God is doing, you need to know how good our Father is and that He only does good things. We sing songs such as "How Great Is Our God," but we must believe that all the time. We must always be in that portal. When friends and family members freak out around you, when you face a disaster or difficulties too insurmountable to deal with, that's when you need to remember that God has prepared good works, and you should walk in them. As a citizen of heaven you are immediately called to put on an eternal perspective as you enter difficult situations, because God is there. He prepared for you to be there, to live and walk by faith in that particular moment. You are a companion with Him to make a difference in earth's environment, and He has provided the portal of heaven for you to activate.

When He says we are His workmanship, that means we were "made appointed"—we were ordained by God to be carriers of His good works on the earth. We are appointed as citizens of kingdom royalty in the earth realm. We abide in Him. We are banded together with Him. We are committed. We are in a place of performing, purpose, and yield. We are His created workmanship with His goodness inside us.

I know you thought you were a total mess, and somebody told you that you're a sinner. But you are His workmanship, royalty, created in Christ Jesus to do good works. You have been redeemed. Whatever was a mess is made right now, and you are carrying it out on earth. Good works are works that benefit and are beautiful. They're valuable and virtuous works. They're honest and worthy works. God created you to do good works, so when you see a terrible thing before you, remember you are walking with power beyond earthly understanding. The earthly realm is programmed to see the negative, to see death, decay, and evil. That's the only way the earth is programmed. It is the curse of the fall of man. But Jesus has redeemed this curse.

GOD CHOSE YOU

When you enter a situation you're inviting what happened to be turned around. That situation needs your faith and action to bring about God's purpose. I honestly don't know why God chooses to use us, but it pleased God that His pure and perfect Son, Jesus Christ, would die for us. That's how important we are to Him. He happened to choose us.

> Ye have not chosen me, but I have chosen you, and ordained you, that ye should go and bring forth fruit, and that your fruit should remain: that whatsoever ye shall ask of the Father in my name, he may give it you.
> —JOHN 15:16

He calls us as royal citizens of heaven, imbued with God's authority to do good works when things look like death or evil. We are love servants of Jesus. We are His companions, and we should enjoy Him while doing good works that He prepared for us to walk in. These works were ordained before any one of them came to be. I don't know about you, but that brings me a lot of peace.

That word *ordained* is the Greek word *tithemi,* broken down to *histemi,* which means to stand, abide, appoint, continue, or covenant.[1] This means these are works He prepared, and He covenants or continues with them because of what Jesus did. Do you know how much power that is? That means goodness is made ready in your hand before you even get to that moment. You might be thinking about how miserable your moment is. If you're facing death, decay, and sickness, that is not the will of the Lord. When you entered that realm of death, the realm was already defeated by Jesus' death and resurrection. Your job is to do the good works God prepared for you to do to change it. You have been made ready to make a difference.

God does not want His people to be subservient to death and decay. Listen, there is so much life inside you. You haven't even begun to enter the portal that holds your eternal prosperous life in its fullness. You haven't even tapped into how smart you are. Your brain cells are popping with eternity.

I know you look in the mirror and see somebody tired, weak, lonely, and sick. That is not the good works He prepared for you to do. Take another look in the mirror and say, "I can do this."

The beloved Son, Jesus, who set you apart, who anointed you, consecrated you, and called you, says, "My son and my daughter, step into the work that I've already prepared for you to do. You will live, and you will bring forth My life for someone else to live. I know someone lied to you and told you that you would die. You will not die. You will live. And you will live forever because I have redeemed your life in past, present, and future."

Today eternity starts when you receive Jesus as your Lord and

Savior. The works you do were made ready in a span of eternity. This is so difficult for us to grasp. We're earthly. We're born into the earth. We sense things on earth. It is like we're split into two different places. The more we come to know the eternal time-frames and operate in heavenly portals, the more we understand the power we walk in and the goodness of our Lord.

It takes some time to grab hold of the truth and power of God's Word. You must wash in the Word of God that you are eternal now and earthly second. I know you thought you were earthly first. But once you received Jesus as your Lord and Savior, you became eternal. That means the earth has got to submit to your eternity. This is why you will not die.

WALK IT OUT

No matter what you're going through, eternity is inside you. It's called a walk because you must walk out your heavenly citizenship until it becomes a reality. This is why Jesus said, "I've given you the ability to tread on snakes and scorpions." He told Joshua (1:3), "Every place that the sole of your foot shall tread upon, that have I given unto you, as I said unto Moses."

This whole thing is about a walk. As I mentioned in a previous chapter, the Greek word for *walk* is *peripateo*. It's made up of a couple of different Greek words, but here's the bottom line. It means to tread around, walk at large as proof of ability. What kind of ability do you have? You have the ability of the eternal realm of heaven inside you. Redemptive power is at your fingertips. When we walk we are showing proof of our eternal ability. This word also means to live. When you walk on the ground you are treading on snakes and scorpions. You are living, and you are stomping on death.

Peripateo also means to deport oneself. What does that

mean? The word *deport* means to behave or carry yourself according to a certain code or standard.[2] It's saying you are a citizen of heaven, so now walk like it, claim the land you were given without question, deport yourself.

You have been put in a position of authority over the earthly realm simply by walking. There's a way of deporting yourself with great dignity. In other words, by the way you carry yourself you establish your land. You are committed to this particular place. You know who you are, and you know what you're doing.

This word *peripateou* is vast; it also means companion,[3] as in being a companion with Jesus. When you walk you're living, you're deporting any alien that's not of the kingdom, and you are taking the land. You are walking as a companion. You are walking with respect to place, cause, or time. In other words, you are saying, "This is my land in this time, and it is complete and taken care of." Why then are you messing with the devil? Why are you all upset? Why is everything so miserable? Why is everything so crazy?

If you can see yourself healed, you're healed. You must walk it out. Yes, it's true. Some people are supernaturally healed in a moment. I witness that all the time, but I witness more bones glowing as people are being changed. Eternity is coming out of their skin. They're living in the worst conditions, but they have the joy of the Lord. They are living in the power of redemption. That's what I see more often.

What do you think makes the devil angrier: somebody walking like that or somebody getting healed in an instant? I tell you, it's the person who's walking it out because that spirit of death says, "No. I told you, you were dead. I told you, you had this disease. I told you, you had this illness." There is more of a fight of faith for one who has to walk out their healing.

A person walking at that level of faith is learning to walk in the same victory that Jesus walked in. When Jesus died on the cross He had to believe in the goodness of His Father. What do you believe to be true about your Father in heaven? What do you believe to be true about Jesus? What do you believe to be true about the Holy Spirit? What do you believe to be true about being redeemed from the curse of death? Until you're tested physically, mentally, and emotionally, you don't even know what's inside you. You don't even know what kind of victory is coming out of your pores.

We need to realize that we are called to walk out this heavenly citizenship on earth. The Israelites walked from Egypt to the Promised Land. They had to walk for forty years. Their feet didn't swell. Their clothes or mantles didn't fall off; they even got water from a rock. Manna came from heaven. They walked that time and distance, and the supernatural of heaven was released.

Today when we read about what the Israelites did and the miracles God performed, these were good works prepared before any one of them came to be. The word in heaven was already written long before the Israelites took that forty-year walk out of bondage. It was already written. It was already done.

Jesus' story was written long before He ever went to the cross.

> And God said, Let us make man in our image, after our likeness: and let them have dominion over the fish of the sea, and over the fowl of the air, and over the cattle, and over all the earth, and over every creeping thing that creepeth upon earth.
>
> —GENESIS 1:26

We live out in earth time the very truths that are already written in eternal time. If you tap into eternal time, let me tell you the kind of miraculous things you will see. God wants miracles and healings to come, but His people must first switch to the heavenly portal of eternity, which will get them on an eternal clock of redemption.

If you want to see the eternal time clock, you must open the heavenly portal and by faith choose to see people from a heavenly perspective of already being complete and whole. Then you call out the truth. You just need to look at somebody and say, "In the name of Jesus, I see that thing on you, but I'm telling you right now, that thing is only in the earthly realm. It's not in the heavenly realm. I see you whole and complete."

A TESTIMONY OF PORTAL BLESSINGS

Let me share when I saw a heavenly portal open, and I could see hope for a young girl. I get the blessing to see into the heavenly realm frequently, as I am a seer prophet and have gone to heaven quite a few times. One weekend I was ministering in Oklahoma, and this amazing encounter happened with a few people who came up for prayer. I could see in the spirit that this one woman had played piano. I asked her, "Do you play an instrument?" She said, "Piano." Well, her fingers were crooked, and I could tell she could not play anymore, but I saw her playing the piano in the spirit realm. We prayed for her fingers, and they began to shift right there and become plump, and her knuckles began to straighten. We spoke the healing from the eternal realm where time was redeemed and where she once played before her hands had swelled.

This ability to see in the heavenly realm while I'm praying for people has happened many times. One woman had been traumatized, and her spine was crooked and her head cocked to the right. I could see her body straighten in the heavenly realm. A portal opened up to me for the redemption of time. This was her body as God saw it before it was broken. When I ministered, the revelation of heaven was present and I called forth what I saw, which was the good work that God wanted to do in this service. She stood straight, her neck rose, and she began to run around the sanctuary.

The last testimony I want to share was a young woman who came to the altar when I was preaching. At the beginning of the service God had me do an altar call for people who were not confident they were saved. A few people came up. Then after I ministered the gospel I just began to preach while they were still there. Suddenly this young girl, who was fourteen years old, came walking up the aisle with two older women who had adopted her. She had death all over her. It was death. I mean, you could see it.

Because of the way she stood at the altar, I stopped preaching. I came over and looked at her, and who I saw was not the person there. I saw the person God sees, the girl before the trauma. All we did was speak to the person that God showed me in the heavenly realm, and that death fell off her in an instant. It took its hands off her. She stood straight. She smiled. She was dressed all in black. I knew this child had been exposed to things that I can't even talk about, but you could just see the death on her. Trauma had held her in bondage, but God redeemed the time.

It came off so much even the pastor who was with me saw it fall off her. I told her to turn around and show those people what she looked like now. She was all lit up; lightness infected every ounce of her darkness. Why? Because a portal of heaven was opened up and the glory was released. It was His goodness and light, and He showed us who she was, and we called that person forth.

We didn't have to do a deliverance of kicking the devil out. He just left her because so much light permeated from the glory around her. God gave us eyes to see who she was from a heavenly standpoint, and we called on that person. Then the enemy let go. There was no fight—just a release of death in an instant.

When you look at somebody in pain, or you have family members living in the dark, do not go fellowship with them in the dark. Do not pet their darkness. Instead call them out into the light and redemption of time. Ask the Lord to show you what heaven sees about them. Open the heavenly portal by faith, and God will be happy to show the good works that He prepared for you to call forth as a citizen of heaven, or call forth into the light.

Look at them and say, "You will come out of that place right now in the name of Jesus. Do not give up the fight." Stand with them, but call out who you see, because who you see at that moment by faith is who God gave you the sight to see in the eternal heavenly realm. That's a portal of eternal good works opening. That's what is written about them in the scrolls of heaven.

People just need your help to do it. When you have the faith to believe that earth time can be turned to eternal time, they can rise from the graveclothes and come into the light. They need somebody. I know the darkness is ugly, and nobody wants to deal with it. Truthfully, you shouldn't be eager to deal with it for prideful purposes, but when you're forced to deal with it, then at least be the one who brings the light. Bring the light; just come on in and make the difference.

You might look like a fool to everybody else. If you can get your head in the eternal realm, you'll be having such a party. They will be wanting to know what Holy Ghost carafe you're drinking from. They will be saying, "Give me just a little bit of that." If you can see through the heavenly portal into the eternal realm, you can manifest this in the earthly realm.

YOU CAN SEE IT

Let's step into a faith strategy for seeing in the spirit. You're called to walk from one space to another. It's already been written for you to walk or tread from eternal heavenly places and spaces into earth realm spaces. Everywhere the soles of your feet tread, you will possess time.

Let me tell you how important this is. You must get beyond earthly time into eternal time. There's nothing more important than shifting your time spheres. Go back and read through chapter 6 again if you need to, because if you don't shift your time spheres, you won't be able to access what's already in existence in the heavenly eternal realm. There it is: already good, whole, righteous, nothing missing, nothing broken. Time has been redeemed by Jesus.

I want you to close your eyes and think about anything irritating you, anything you want to see changed on earth, anything that needs to be redeemed and made whole. We've all got something that we look at and say, "I wish it looked different. I want to see a difference." Once you grab hold of that in your mind, you see pain in the earthly realm. You see something missing or broken, something lost or hopeless. It may be sickness. It may be death. It has lack and poverty and is not whole or complete or may even be unfinished. It has one of those components to it. Look at it as a picture in your mind. What you are seeing is on earth.

Ask the Lord to open the heavenly portal into the eternal realm. Tell Him you want to see His eternal heavenly viewpoint of it. Tell Him you want to see in a picture what the eternal scrolls already say about this situation. The portal is open now. So look again, but this time see it being made whole or complete. You know what it would look like if it were not broken or missing or in lack or poverty. In the mighty name of Jesus, see it from this perspective. Rest right there in the eternal perspective, the heavenly perspective, God's perspective. Wash it in the blood of Jesus. Wash it in holiness. Wash it in purity and righteousness right now. Wash it in everything you want it to be by washing it in love and faith. Wash it in hope.

Then say, "Father, I thank You for changing my spiritual sight and vision right now to see into the eternal time zone." In this heavenly portal, which opens into an eternal realm, you are now seeing the real story that was written. You might be thinking about your family members, friends, or finances. You might be wondering why something has gone on for so long and hasn't stopped yet. Whatever that situation is, see it in the eternal as you see purpose and destiny. See it as Ezekiel saw it, as explained in chapter 4. Hold on to purpose and destiny.

I believe what you see in the eternal is what you have right now on earth! The Lord says it's done. It's finished. It's complete. It's final. It's final right now in the name of Jesus. Get a good picture in your mind. Get an accurate picture in your mind. Let it burn into your brain cells. Let it burn into your soul right now. This is very important because God says it will happen. He will make it exactly as you see it. That's what He told me. He said, "Tell them I will make it exactly as they see it right now in the name of Jesus."

FAITH ACTIVATION

Here's a word of wisdom. You have a picture burning in your brain right now of heavenly perspective, the eternal realm of truth. Note in your journal the day, the time, the moment, and write what you saw, because now you've got to walk it out as if it's done. You must tread this out with words of faith. Then it's complete. Do not go back in prayers to that language you had before you started this faith activation. God says it's done. Your prayers will be different about it now. There will be more prayers of "Thank You, Lord, for doing this thing on earth!"

Walk it out in faith, as it was prepared to be a good work made manifest in this earth realm right now. It's already done in the eternal time zone of truth. It's total, nothing missing, nothing broken, complete, and shalom. It is redeemed by Jesus' blood sacrifice, resurrection, and ascension. When we hold on to what He told us, we enter the eternal realm. Your faith has to stay at that level because the enemy comes to sift your faith. May your faith not fail you right now, in the mighty name of Jesus. Stand firm, and you will see it come to pass. It is done! Worship the Lord in thanksgiving!

In closing, my prayer for you is that everything you read in this book will come alive to you in your spiritual senses and that you will forever be changed by understanding that eternal time is living and active right now—and you are walking it out in earthly time. Jesus has redeemed the curse and bought back eternal time. You have received the blessing from His sacrifice, resurrection, and ascension. I believe the impartation from this book will bring forth a new way of seeing your world on earth. You will never be the same since time has been redeemed and you have learned the keys to walking it out. You are victorious in every way!

QUESTIONS for REFLECTION

1. What was it that you saw by spiritual sight in faith within the heavenly portal to the eternal realm?

2. Write out a prayer of thanksgiving. Let this be a continual prayer until what you saw in the spirit is made manifest on earth.

3. What can you do to discipline your mind to see in the spirit from the perspective that time has been redeemed for everything in life?

Final Prayer for Salvation

I KNOW YOU LEARNED a lot from this book, and I would love to connect with you. Please read on for how to reach out to me. If you have not yet received Jesus as your Lord and Savior, now is a great time to do this. Jesus is the reason we have dominion power. He's the reason revealed in the New Testament, or new covenant of grace. If you want to know Jesus, all you have to do is believe in your heart and confess with your mouth that Jesus Christ is your Lord and Savior. Pray a prayer like this:

> *Father, I believe right now in my heart that Jesus came to save me from my sin, eternal death, and the grave. The Bible says in Romans 10:9–13 (NIV) that "if you declare with your mouth, 'Jesus is Lord,' and believe in your heart that God raised him from the*

dead, you will be saved. For it is with your heart that you believe and are justified, and it is with your mouth that you profess your faith and are saved. As Scripture says, 'Anyone who believes in him will never be put to shame.' For there is no difference between Jew and Gentile—the same Lord is Lord of all and richly blesses all who call on him, for, 'Everyone who calls on the name of the Lord will be saved.'"

Then ask Him to fill you with the power of the Holy Spirit, because that's what He wants to do.

Father, I thank You that veils were removed from my eyes and I can see the revelation in Your Word. I ask You, Lord, to quicken my spiritual senses of seeing, hearing, smelling, tasting, and touching You everywhere. I thank You, Lord, that Your work is finished on the cross and mine is just beginning as a kingdom citizen, a member of the royal priesthood, to follow after the things of God. I thank You that You can keep me from falling and preserve my soul until the end. Lord, help me see into the supernatural and bring that into the natural. I want to commune with You every day! Amen!

Please share this book with a friend who needs encouragement. I have prayed over this book and hope that you have been changed by reading it. I believe not only that God touched you through it but that you will continue to read it for years to come as a reminder of the royal citizen you are. Please contact my ministry at info@candicesmithyman.com, as I would like to know who you are and how this book has changed you.

For further information on salvation and the baptism of the Holy Spirit, visit my website at www.candicesmithyman.com, and go to the "School of Supernatural" or the "Shop" button for resources.

Notes

PREFACE

1. Bible Hub, s.v. *"shalom,"* accessed November 4, 2021, https://biblehub.com/hebrew/7965.htm.

INTRODUCTION

1. Bible Study Tools, s.v. *"dunamis,"* accessed 10/11/21, https://www.biblestudytools.com/lexicons/greek/nas/dunamis.html.

CHAPTER 1

1. Bible Study Tools, s.v. *"'eth,"* accessed October 12, 2021, https://www.biblestudytools.com/lexicons/hebrew/nas/eth.html.
2. Bible Study Tools, s.v. *"'ad,"* accessed October 12, 2021, https://www.biblestudytools.com/lexicons/hebrew/nas/ad-2.html.
3. QuotesCosmos, s.v. "the world," accessed October 12, 2021, https://www.quotescosmos.com/bible/bible-verses/Ecclesiastes-3-11-He-has-made-everything-beautiful.html.
4. Bible Study Tools, s.v. *"muwth,"* accessed October 12, 2021, https://www.biblestudytools.com/lexicons/hebrew/nas/muwth.html .
5. Bible Tools, s.v. *"radaph,"* accessed October 12, 2021, https://www.bibletools.org/index.cfm/fuseaction/Lexicon.show/ID/H7291/radaph.htm.

CHAPTER 2

1. Bible Study Tools, s.v. *"anabaino,"* accessed October 12, 2021, https://www.biblestudytools.com/lexicons/greek/nas/anabaino.html.
2. Bible Study Tools, s.v. *"anabaino."*
3. Dictionary.com, s.v. "portal," accessed October 12, 2021, https://www.dictionary.com/browse/portal.
4. Dictionary.com, s.v. "realm," accessed October 12, 2021, https://www.dictionary.com/browse/realm.

CHAPTER 3

1. Bible Study Tools, s.v. "*hegeomai,*" accessed October 25, 2021, https://www.biblestudytools.com/lexicons/greek/nas/hegeomai.html.
2. Candice Smithyman, *Releasing Heaven: Creating Supernatural Environments Through Heavenly Encounters* (Shippensburg, PA: Destiny Image, 2020).

CHAPTER 4

1. Got Questions, s.v. "*shalom,*" accessed October 26, 2021, https://www.gotquestions.org/Shalom-meaning.html .
2. Bible Study Tools, s.v. "*katartizo,*" accessed October 27, 2021, https://www.biblestudytools.com/lexicons/greek/nas/katartizo.html .
3. QuotesCosmos, s.v. "*haya,*" accessed October 27, 2021, https://www.quotescosmos.com/bible/bible-concordance/H2421.html.
4. QuotesCosmos, s.v. "*yada,*" accessed October 27, 2021, https://www.quotescosmos.com/bible/bible-concordance/H3045.html .
5. Bible Study Tools, s.v. "*yabesh,*" accessed October 27, 2021, https://www.biblestudytools.com/lexicons/hebrew/kjv/yabesh.html.
6. QuotesCosmos, s.v. "*naba,*" accessed October 27, 2021, https://www.quotescosmos.com/bible/bible-concordance/H5012.html.
7. Compelling Truth, s.v. "*ruach,*" accessed October 27, 2021, https://www.compellingtruth.org/meaning-ruach.html.
8. Blue Letter Bible, s.v. "*qol,*" accessed October 28, 2021, https://www.blueletterbible.org/lexicon/h6963/kjv/wlc/0-1/.

CHAPTER 5

1. You can learn more about my e-course at www.charismacourses.com.

CHAPTER 6

1. Bible Study Tools, s.v. "*hupostatis,*" accessed October 28, 2021, https://www.biblestudytools.com/lexicons/greek/kjv/hupostasis.html.
2. Bible Study Tools, s.v. "*basileia,*" accessed October 29, 2021, https://www.biblestudytools.com/lexicons/greek/nas/basileia.html.

3. Bible Study Tools, s.v. "*basileus*," accessed October 29, 2021, https://www.biblestudytools.com/lexicons/greek/nas/basileus.html.

4. Bible Study Tools, s.v. "basis," accessed October 29, 2021, https://www.biblestudytools.com/lexicons/greek/nas/basis.html.

CHAPTER 7

1. George Lamsa, *Holy Bible: From the Ancient Eastern Text* (San Francisco: HarperCollins, 1985).

2. Bible Study Tools, s.v. "*basileia*," accessed November 1, 2021, https://www.biblestudytools.com/lexicons/greek/nas/basileia.html.

3. Candice Smithyman, *Soul Transformation: Your Personal Journey* (Shippensburg, PA: Destiny Image, 2018).

4. Bible Study Tools, s.v. "*phren*," accessed November 1, 2021, https://www.biblestudytools.com/lexicons/greek/nas/phren.html.

5. Bible Study Tools, s.v. "phrasso," accessed November 1, 2021, https://www.biblestudytools.com/lexicons/greek/nas/phrasso.html.

6. QuotesCosmos, s.v. "*politeuma*," accessed November 1, 2021, https://www.quotescosmos.com/bible/bible-concordance/G4175.html.

CHAPTER 8

1. Bible Study Tools, s.v. "*kaphaph*," accessed November 1, 2021, https://www.biblestudytools.com/lexicons/hebrew/kjv/kaphaph.html.

2. Bible Study Tools, s.v. "*regel*," accessed November 1, 2021, https://www.biblestudytools.com/lexicons/hebrew/nas/regel.html.

3. Bible Study Tools, s.v. "*darak*," accessed November 1, 2021, https://www.biblestudytools.com/lexicons/hebrew/nas/darak.html.

4. Bible Study Tools, s.v. "*paripateo*," accessed November 1, 2021, https://www.biblestudytools.com/lexicons/greek/nas/peripateo.html.

5. Bible Study Tools, s.v. "*peri*," accessed November 1, 2021, https://www.biblestudytools.com/lexicons/greek/nas/peri.html.

6. Bible Study Tools, s.v. *"pateo,"* accessed November 1, 2021, https://www.biblestudytools.com/lexicons/greek/nas/pateo.html.

7. Smithyman, *Soul Transformation.*

CHAPTER 10

1. Bible Study Tools, s.v. *"histemi,"* accessed November 4, 2021, https://www.biblestudytools.com/lexicons/greek/nas/histemi.html.

2. Bible Study Tools, s.v. *"paripateo."*

3. Bible Study Tools, s.v. *"paripateo."*